THE ROSES OF EYAM

A Play

DON TAYLOR

SAMUEL  FRENCH

LONDON
NEW YORK   TORONTO   SYDNEY   HOLLYWOOD

ISBN 0 573 11386 6

CHARACTERS

William Mompesson, Rector of Eyam
Sir George Saville, his patron
Catherine Mompesson, his wife
His Two Small Children
The Bedlam
Old Unwin
Andrew Merril
Marshall Howe
Thomas Stanley, former Rector of Eyam during the
    Commonwealth
Rowland Torre, from the next village
George Vicars, the village tailor
Colonel Bradshaw, the local squire
Mrs Bradshaw
A Carter, from London

A Boy	**Isaac Thornley**
	Edward Thornley
Mrs Cooper	**Elizabeth Thornley**
Edward Cooper	**William Thornley**
Jonathan Cooper	**Francis Thornley**
	Mary Thornley
Mrs Sydall	
Richard Sydall	**George Frith**
Emmot Sydall	**Frances Frith**
Ellen Sydall	**Mary Frith**
Sarah Sydall	**Francis Frith**
John Sydall	**Ann Frith**
	Thomas Frith
Humphrey Torre	**Elizabeth Frith**
Edytha Torre	
William Torre	**John Wilson**
John Torre	**Deborah Wilson**
Alice Torre	
Scythe Torre	**Elizabeth Swanne**
Thomas Torre	
Frances Torre	**Lydia Chapman**
Mrs Hancock	**Rowland Mower**
John Hancock	**George Mower**
William Hancock	
Alice Hancock	
Elizabeth Hancock	

The Play was first performed at The Northcott Theatre, Exeter, on September 23rd, 1970, by members of The Northcott Theatre Company

Designed by Saul Radomsky
Directed by Anton Rodgers

The Play begins in August 1665, and ends in October 1666

"Ring a ring of roses,
A pocketful of posies,
A-tishoo, a-tishoo
All fall down"

To my Mother and Father, with thanks

ACT I*

The set is a representation of the Derbyshire village of Eyam, in the seventeenth century. In a central position is a large Saxon cross, based on the cross in Eyam churchyard, with an open area round it

The setting must be flexible enough to be able to contain scenes located in various parts of the village, principally, the interior of the rectory, interiors of several Eyam cottages, the church, the open place round the cross where the villagers meet, areas of hillside around the village, and in Act III the little valley known as The Delf. The set must be designed to be permanent, so that each scene can flow continuously into the next without interruption

While the CURTAIN *is down, music begins. When it rises, we see a silhouette, the village and the cross. Sir George Saville enters, followed by William Mompesson. They are both wearing travelling-clothes. The music stops*

Saville Well, Mompesson? What does it feel like?
Mompesson What?
Saville Responsibility.
Mompesson Gratifying.
Saville I suppose I should have guessed you'd say that.
Mompesson I've waited ten years for today. I was sixteen when I promised myself to God's service. Ten years of hard study.

A pause. Mompesson looks round

  It's small.
Saville Big enough for a beginner. You couldn't ask more of a first living.
Mompesson I'm grateful, of course. But I did hope . . .
Saville What? London?
Mompesson Lesser men have done it.
Saville I believe you. But if you're the man I think you are, your time here won't be wasted. I haven't done it without thought.
Mompesson I realize that.
Saville Ten years of Cambridge would suffice in a world made of books. But scholarship isn't enough. You're in the world now, not your study. You must become a man among men.
Mompesson A man of God among men.
Saville But men, not fellow scholars. Lead miners, copper workers, coopers, fieldsmen, tanners, men to whom words are drawings, and whose crosses you must witness. It will be a real test, William, don't undervalue it.
Mompesson No.

Saville You'll be unpopular at first.

Mompesson Why?

Saville Your age, your learning. Your religion, too, in these parts.

Mompesson What do you mean?

Saville You're too young to remember the war. Many of those wounds are still open; some are festering.

Mompesson I remember what it was like before the King came back. And the war, too, when I was a boy.

Saville But you didn't see the dying, and you don't know the bitterness. You've heard me speak of Thomas Stanley?

Mompesson Yes.

Saville He was rector here under Cromwell. Calls himself a Nonconformist, which means he knows better how to worship God than God does. He's still here.

Mompesson I didn't know that.

Saville There are about three hundred and fifty people in this village. Perhaps two hundred of them are still his friends; which means that they're your enemies.

Mompesson The rector of God has no enemies, only sheep to be fed.

Saville Now rinse that starch from your face, my boy, I know my duty and you know yours. But you must come two steps down from heaven if you want to speak to these people. The lead miners in these parts were strong Parliament men, some of them the most fanatic. You'll have to make some concessions.

Mompesson Concessions? Do you know what made me a churchman?

Saville Your father's good example, and your own intelligence.

Mompesson No. My intelligence could have made me a civil servant or a diplomat. I could have spent my life making the King laugh and getting drunk. I chose Christ because of a vision.

Saville God preserve me from Visions. What do you mean?

Mompesson In Eyam I shall lay the first foundation of God's house. The drawing is clear in my mind, and I won't begin by making concessions to the material.

Saville laughs

Why are you laughing at me?

Saville To bring you back to earth, my boy. You won't see anything from a pedestal looking down.

Mompesson I don't intend to be remote. But you know I have had little experience of people of this kind.

Saville My dear William . . .

Mompesson Yes, I know, it is a failing in me, I am conscious of it. My life has been scholarly, but I shall learn. I think it important that I should establish my position from the start.

Saville So do I, too, and I don't doubt you will soon become dearly loved here. They are God-fearing people in Eyam. There is nothing beyond their reach, if you are their signpost.

Mompesson To the best of my ability, I shall be that and more.

Catherine Mompesson enters, with her two small Children, aged four and five

Saville Here's your wife, they must be finished at the coach. Is it all unloaded?

Catherine Yes, it's done. Isn't this a beautiful place? Shut away in the hills, so you'd never know it was there.

Saville The most beautiful village in Derbyshire, so the locals say. For myself, I'd call it pretty bleak. But not aloud.

Mompesson It's strange the way the road seems to wind up through the cliff face. It makes it even more isolated. Is there no other way?

Saville There's a road across the high moor to Sheffield, if you have a good thick cloak and a taste for solitude. Shall we go in?

A thin, tinkling bell is heard off

Mompesson What's that noise?

They listen for a second as the bell gets closer

The Bedlam enters. He is a mental defective, dressed in rags, carrying a tin box for pennies, which he rattles, and wearing a small silver bell about his neck. He is about twenty, tall and thin, with a large bony head, and a vacant stare. He stoops and limps, dragging one foot on a twisted ankle. He stops when he sees the three strangers

There is a pause. The Bedlam rattles the tin box very loudly, and then hobbles over to them, and stands holding out the box and looking at them

Saville Hallo, boy. How much have you got in your box today?

Bedlam Give me a penny.

Saville There.

Bedlam I collect pennies. I like the old black ones best. I polish them up till all the heads are shiny.

Saville What do you buy with them?

Bedlam I throw them in the stream and watch them turning over till they reach the waterfall. The little ones always win. Have you got any little ones?

Mompesson I think so . . .

Bedlam You have to make them shiny, or you can't see them in the water.

Mompesson Who is he?

Saville No-one knows where he came from. He sleeps in a hut outside the village.

Catherine Poor boy. How does he live?

Saville By begging. He's very friendly, and always cheerful, in spite of his bent bones and empty mind. Aren't you, boy?

Bedlam I can tell fortunes.

Saville They stand him on a platform every year at the Harvest Wake, and he tells people by their clothes and the shape of their faces. He forecasts the weather too, don't you, boy?

Bedlam This winter will be cold, but in spring it will get hot again.

Saville That's a fair bet.

Catherine It's cruel to make him a plaything. Come here, boy.

Bedlam Hallo, lady.

Catherine You'll need a new coat before the winter, or you'll be cold.

Bedlam I don't feel the cold.

Catherine You haven't much choice, I suppose. You come to the rectory
tomorrow and we'll find you a new coat.

Saville Tell our fortunes for us, boy.

Catherine Don't make fun of him.

Saville No, he likes it. Go on, boy, begin with me.

Bedlam You will always be a fat man.

Saville Me! I'm not fat!

Bedlam Until December.

Saville And what happens then?

Bedlam They polish your bones and hang them up in the cupboard. And
all your warm clothes . . .

Saville What about them?

Bedlam Will be left in a pile on the floor.

Saville You see? He enjoys it.

Bedlam You're all dressed in black.

Mompesson It's the colour of my calling.

Bedlam Black is a sad colour, and you must always wear it in the churchyard.

Catherine What about me? Tell me a nice fortune, and I'll give you another
penny.

Bedlam Roses must be pruned at the end of the summer. Merril told me
that.

Catherine Who's Merril?

Saville An old man who lives on the edge of the village. The boy helps him
in his garden.

Catherine Haven't you got anything for me except garden stories?

Bedlam No, lady. Nothing at all.

Saville Run along now, boy, you must go back to your hut, or you'll be
out in the dark. We'd better go in, too, if the baggage is ready. Come on,
children.

Bedlam I'll catch a mole to do the digging.

Saville Of course you will.

Saville exits with the two Children

Bedlam follows, and turns at the exit

Bedlam Good-bye, Blackman. Good-bye, rose.

Bedlam exits

Catherine Poor boy. We must try to help him.

Mompesson is away from her in thought

What's wrong?
Mompesson Nothing.
Catherine Tell me.
Mompesson This place.
Catherine I'm sure we shall be happy here.
Mompesson A simple man, whose faith is by the book, could give these people all they need. Do you think I can? What language shall I speak to pitmen and carters and barrel-makers, to farmers who dig themselves insensible all day, and snore their nights through without one thought or dream of God? They don't need signposts from me, or anyone. They want a comforter, a spiritual shoe-horn to ease them through their lives. I shall bless their children, marry them, and bury them. They'll come to me for herbs for their sick wives, water on their babies' foreheads, and prayers and crosses for their dying grandfathers. My most important office will be president of the churchyard, the man who keeps the toll gate to heaven.
Catherine You must silence those thoughts. The voice of ambition isn't wanted here, only the voice of love. You know it in your heart.
Mompesson The knowledge is one thing. The action another. I hope I know my failings. I didn't think they would be put to the test so soon.

Mompesson looks at her for a second, and they leave together

The Lights come up a few points, and the whole stage is used for the Harvest Wake scene. Music begins to play

Simultaneously, three people enter. Up C, *Marshall Howe, an enormous man, well over six feet, built like Samson. Andrew Merril enters* L *and Old Unwin* R; *two querulous and lively old men, both about eighty. The two old men stop when they see each other*

Unwin Good day, Andrew Merril.
Merril Good day, Unwin.

They both turn briskly and begin to leave the way they have come. Howe comes downstage to form the apex of a triangle

Howe For God's sake, is that all?

The two old men stop and turn

Nothing else for the feast day?

They both walk over to him

Unwin You're a blasphemer, Marshall Howe, good afternoon.
Merril Take not the Lord's name in vain, good afternoon.
Howe My penance is to make you friends.
Unwin I spoke to him last wake day.
Merril So did I.

Unwin I said "Good day, Merril".
Merril I said "Good day, Unwin".
Unwin Enough idle chat for one year.
Merril Quite enough!

*At this point the stage begins to fill with people, the villagers, who will act
as the Chorus. Their main purpose in the play is to diminish, thus creating
a visual image of the whole play*

*The Chorus consists of five families, which we are conscious of as family
units, and which should be emphasised as such by the Director, and various
other villagers necessary at various points in the action. These numbers
should be added to, or even subtracted from, according to the size of the stage
available. The point is simply that the stage for this first scene should be full
of a large and animated crowd of people*

*The families come on simultaneously from different parts of the stage,
bringing various props with them, to suggest the fair, at the Director's
discretion, remembering only that an autumn fair in a country village is
a mixture of a celebratory and a commercial occasion. They are all on
stage, and the stage is fully dressed when the following section ends*

*The villagers are as follows: the Sydalls: Mrs Sydall and Richard,
parents, middle aged; John, aged sixteen; Sarah, aged seventeen; Ellen,
aged eighteen, and Emmot, aged twenty*

*The Hancocks: Mrs Hancock and John, parents, middle aged; William, a
brother, aged thirty-eight; Alice, aged twenty-five, and Elizabeth, aged
twenty*

*The Friths: Frances, mother, aged forty-five; George, father, aged fifty;
Elizabeth, sister, aged forty-four; Mary, aged twenty-five; Francis, aged
twenty-three; Ann, aged twenty, and Thomas, aged nineteen*

*The Torres: Humphrey, grandfather, aged seventy-five; Edytha, grand-
mother, aged sixty-five; William, father, aged forty-four; Alice, mother,
aged forty-two; John, aged twenty-seven; Scythe, aged twenty-one;
Thomas, aged eighteen, and Frances, aged seventeen*

*The Thornleys: Isaac, grandfather, aged eighty; Edward, father, aged
fifty-five; Elizabeth, mother, aged fifty-six; William, aged thirty-five;
Francis, aged twenty-eight, and Mary, aged twenty-five*

*John and Deborah Wilson, aged thirty-five and forty; Elizabeth Swanne,
aged twenty; Lydia Chapman, aged forty-two; Rowland and George
Mower, aged forty-five and thirty; George Vicars, a tailor, aged about
thirty; Mrs Cooper, middle aged, and Edward and Jonathan Cooper,
thirtyish and mid-twenties*

The dialogue between the three men continues uninterrupted as the villagers begin to enter

Howe Not for today. This is Harvest Sunday, fit time for sermons, and the text is age, so listen. Age is the time when a man's life becomes a circle, when grandfather begins to toddle again, and old men have so much snow on their heads their brains turn to water. True?

Unwin True.

Merril True.

Howe A time when coffins stand open, and spades are called for, and old men need prayers. True?

Merril True.

Howe A time for totting accounts, balancing books, and settling old scores. True?

Unwin True.

Merril True.

Howe How did it all start?

Unwin How old are you this year, Merril?

Merril Eighty.

Unwin Liar! Seventy-nine!

Merril I remember the day the old Queen died.

Unwin I remember the Armada.

Merril I fought the Armada!

Howe Boys were men in those days.

Merril And I was first with Joan Dunnett.

Unwin But it was me she preferred.

Merril I proposed on top of a haystack.

Unwin I was listening at the bottom. She said no.

Howe Which one did she choose?

Merril Neither.

Unwin She married a shoemaker from Sheffield.

Merril Twenty-one children.

Unwin Sixty-eight grandchildren.

Merril Died of a broken heart.

Unwin And senile decay.

Merril Forty years old.

Unwin Sixteen hundred and twenty-five!

Merril Before the war.

Unwin Years ago . . .

Howe And you're both still here, like the old leavings of last year's dinner. There's just time for a truce, before you get cleared away.

Rowland Torre enters upstage, as the three men join the crowd. He is a young man of twenty, a sturdy and tough-looking hill farmer from the neighbouring village

At the end of the above dialogue, the Sydall family have isolated themselves from the main crowd, and interest switches to them as Sarah is the first to see Rowland

Sarah Sydall Rowland!

Ellen Sydall Emmot, it's Rowland!

Rowland joins them

Richard Sydall Hallo, Rowland, how are you?

Rowland Hallo, Mr Sydall, fine thanks.

Richard Sydall Good harvest?

Rowland All in. Hallo, Emmot.

Emmot Hallo, Rowland.

Mrs Sydall Were you at church this morning, Rowland?

Rowland Yes, Mrs Sydall.

Mrs Sydall Did you pray hard for God's blessing on the two of you?
Marriage isn't a thing to be taken lightly.

Rowland Very hard, Mrs Sydall.

Mrs Sydall Good lad.

The Bedlam enters and stands looking at the people

Ellen Sydall Everyone's here, Rowland, celebrating the harvest.

Sarah Sydall No, they've all come to see the engagement.

John Sydall There's the Hancocks come down from Riley.

Ellen Sydall And all your cousins Torre.

Rowland I knew they were coming.

Sarah Sydall Scythe and Thomas have brought their pipes for the dancing.

Mrs Sydall They shouldn't be dancing on a Sunday!

Richard Sydall Why not? It's a day of rest, not a day of misery. There's
always dancing when there's an engagement on wakes day.

Mrs Sydall I still don't hold with it. It's disrespectful on the Lord's day.

Richard Sydall No more than all your women's gossip. I heard you this
morning after church. "The rector's wife, Mrs Frith, she's that thin and
ill looking . . ."

Mrs Sydall Well, so she is, it's the truth.

Richard Sydall Far more malicious than any dancing, so you can turn a
blind eye for once. Come on, Rowland, let's see what you can do. Man
and wife who can't dance when the time calls won't live long.

Rowland Do you mind, Emmot?

Emmot I don't mind.

*The two Torres begin to play, Emmot and Rowland begin to dance together,
and are soon followed by other younger couples*

Mrs Sydall You'll see my daughter dead and in Hell with all your wild
games of a Sunday.

Richard Sydall You've seen plenty of games of your own in your day, old
Sarah.

Mrs Sydall Well!

*By this time most of the younger ones have joined in the dancing, while the
older ones stand in a half-circle, shouting encouragement and clapping to the
music, or joining in themselves. The Bedlam watches them. He is joined by
Marshall Howe*

Colonel Bradshaw enters, with Mrs Bradshaw, looking very much lord of the manor

Howe Hallo, boy. Have you come to join in the dancing?

Bedlam All the people.

Howe They're all here today: Squire Bradshaw, wearing a festive smile, and wondering how much it's costing him, the hardworking family Frith, still in their fieldboots, and all the starched-up Thornleys, enjoying a thin religious pleasure, suitable for Sunday. Even George Vicars the tailor, leaving his scissors and moneybags for one afternoon. Let them dance, eh boy? It'll be winter soon.

Bedlam I can't dance with my legs.

Howe You're an old ragbag, aren't you, boy, an old ragbag full of junk and rubbish.

Bedlam I can dance with my head, though.

Howe What, is there dancing in there? All I can see in your eyes, boy, is sky, and blue clouds.

Bedlam My dancing goes on forever, and never gets tired.

Howe One of the big advantages of being a madman.

Thomas Stanley enters. He is a rather down-at-heel-looking Puritan preacher in his fifties, an imposing man with a mane of white hair, seeming to bring on the stage with him, in his very appearance, a memory of the Puritan revolution at its most positive and idealistic stage. He is a big rugged man, more at home in the market place than in the study, a man of intensity and imagination, with none of the narrow-gutted and repressive qualities of nineteenth-century Puritanism. He is brother to John Milton and Gerrard Winstanley, and shares their vision, even if at this point in the play bitterness seems to have defeated him

Stanley stands for a moment watching the dancing, then turns away. Edward Thornley detaches himself from his family and crosses over to him

Edward Thornley Good afternoon, Mr Stanley.

Stanley This is a sad sight, Edward Thornley.

Edward Thornley Ay, a sad sight for the Lord's day. But my people know their duty. There was none of this when you were rector here.

Stanley It will have to be paid for.

Edward Thornley Times have changed in five years. But some of us still keep faith. Why don't you speak to them. They will still listen to you.

Stanley It is no longer my place to speak.

Edward Thornley More's the pity. Have you met the new King's man?

Stanley No.

Edward Thornley You've missed nothing. A youngster, full of arrogance and spleen, who spits in the dust as we pass.

Stanley I've no wish to meet him. Our ways are opposite.

Edward Thornley Some of us fought for the Parliament once. We can fight for God now, if you speak out for us.

Stanley I can do nothing now.

Edward Thornley Don't leave us, Minister. We need you.

Stanley I can pray for you. We can meet in your houses and talk together. Other than that we can only wait. God's hand is still on the wheel. Those who are up now will be brought down, and the downtrodden will stand. We must be patient, and love God.

Stanley and Edward Thornley go upstage together to the Thornley group. Various people acknowledge Stanley as he goes. He replies, but retiringly. He has no wish to be the centre of interest. The dancing continues for a few seconds

Mompesson enters downstage and absorbs the scene

Edward Thornley nudges Stanley, and Stanley turns and sees Mompesson. Mompesson becomes conscious of his gaze, and the two men look at each other. The musicians stop playing when they see what is happening, the dancing gradually ceases, and everyone becomes conscious of the imminent meeting of the two men. Mompesson begins to make a move towards Stanley, and immediately Stanley moves diagonally away from him through the crowd. As he gets clear of the crowd Mompesson calls to him

Mompesson Mr Stanley.

Slowly Stanley turns to face him. The villagers gaze avidly

Stanley Sir?

Mompesson William Mompesson . . .

Mompesson moves over to Stanley, with his arm extended to shake hands. Stanley ignores it and looks at him

Stanley Good afternoon.

Mompesson is rather taken aback, but he has decided to be friendly in a formal manner

Mompesson I have been looking forward—ever since I arrived—to meeting you. But I have been unable to find out where you are living now.

Stanley Not surprising, sir. I live by begging, on the charitable crumbs of those tables that still have a place set for me. I have no house, no land, no Church, but the oak tree at the end of the street. You can always find me there.

Mompesson I have been meaning to ask you to dine with me at the rectory.

Stanley You can spare the trouble.

Mompesson No trouble, I assure you . . .

Stanley I left that house five years ago on the arms of the King's soldiers. If I ever return to it, it won't be as a guest.

Mompesson Times have changed, Mr Stanley, and the law is the law. I suppose we must disagree, but we need not be enemies.

Stanley You are a scholar, sir?

Mompesson Like a good workman, I have studied my trade.

Stanley Then you will have learned that there is right and wrong, and that oil and vinegar in the same jar won't mix without a beating. You build your palace, and I will build mine, and let God decide which of us has constructed a tomb. My thanks for your kindness, sir. Good afternoon.

Stanley turns and leaves

Mompesson stands for a moment looking at the crowd. They watch him in silence

Mompesson seems about to say something, but suddenly turns and goes out

Chatter breaks out among the crowd, but it is restrained by what they have just seen. The musicians begin to play again, but no-one dances. Edward Thornley and George Frith join Marshall Howe downstage

Howe There's a black cloud gone over the sun. There'll be no more dancing today.

Edward Thornley He didn't say much for himself, did he.

George Frith The new rector?

Edward Thornley Won't lower himself to speak to us.

George Frith He's no great love for us, if the truth's known.

Howe Did you hear a rumble like an earthquake?

George Frith No.

Howe It was the dead men of a war twenty years old turning in their graves. They get restless in their sheets at that kind of talk, and their fingerbones feel for weapons. Some of the living too, eh Edward?

Edward Thornley I was at Marston Moor, and proud to have been there.

Howe But the Good Old Cause is dead, and its soldiers gone rotten. And those that are left are poor shells, scooped out and brittle. Like our once rector Stanley.

Edward Thornley What do you mean by that? The Minister is——

George Frith (*cutting in*) Those times are best forgotten.

Howe Try telling your churchmen that.

Richard Sydall Ay, those fellows will still be fighting, even on my daughter's engagement day.

Edward Thornley Some things, Richard Sydall, are worth fighting for.

Richard Sydall Ay, I daresay, Edward Thornley, I daresay. Nevertheless, all men are welcome at my house to drink my daughter's health, however they choose to say their prayers.

George Frith Say amen to that, Edward.

Edward Thornley Amen. With all my heart.

Richard Sydall If we can find her, that is! They've both wandered off some road so that the Lord knows where they've got to!

The Carter enters. He is carrying a large black wooden box. He sees the three men and goes to them

Carter Is this the village of Eyam?

Howe You must have driven a long way if you don't know that.

Carter I have. I need a rest and a drink.

Edward Thornley Where are you from?

Carter London.

George Frith London!

Howe Strangers are rare enough here. If you're from London you're almost unique.

Edward Thornley What's the news in the south?

Carter Not good.

George Frith More troubles?

Carter Not the sort of news to be talking about.

Howe Then don't talk about it. What have you got in the box?

Carter Merchandise. Can you show me to the house of a Mr Vicars?

Edward Thornley George Vicars the tailor?

Carter That'll be the one.

George Frith He shares a cottage with the Coopers. But you needn't carry it, he's here. George!

Howe George Vicars! Here's a present for you, from London!

George Vicars comes over to them from the main crowd. He is a small and rather fussy little man of about thirty

Vicars Ah, my box, my box, my box. Good. Is it all there?

Carter How should I know, I haven't looked.

Vicars From the big drapers in Thames Street?

Carter That's it.

Howe What is it, George, solid gold?

Carter Heavy enough. My horses are half dead.

Vicars All in good time you shall know. You shall know all in good time.

Carter I need a good meal.

Howe He'll give you some bread and cheese if you're lucky.

Vicars Pick it up and bring it over to the cross.

George Frith Are you going back tonight?

Carter Not to London, I'm not.

Edward Thornley You're not going back?

Carter Not this year.

Vicars leads the Carter, carrying the box, over to the cross. Vicars stands on the pedestal of the cross, and the people gather round to see what is happening

Vicars Ladies and gentlemen of Eyam! I have a very important announcement to make.

Cheers and jeers from the assembling crowd, "What is it, George", etc., etc.

A piece of very good news for the people of this village. You see here a large black box ...

Howe His grandmother's coffin, he's putting her up for auction.

More cheers

Vicars Nothing of the kind. There's no rubbish in this box, I'll tell you that!

Richard Sydall Come on, George, don't keep us in suspense!

Vicars There's nothing but the latest fashions in there! There's London clothes, and at Eyam prices! First comers get best choice!

John Wilson Let's see them then, George, why not start now?

Vicars Tomorrow will be soon enough. Nine o'clock at Mrs Cooper's.

Howe He needs time to work out his percentages and profits, don't you, George?

George Mower Why are they so cheap, George? Did you get them from the rubbish dump?

Francis Frith You cut them from the corpses on the gallows, didn't you, George.

Vicars You'll find out tomorrow. Laugh if you like, Francis Frith. You come early tomorrow, and you'll get a surprise.

Cheers from the crowd

Let's go down to Mrs Cooper's, and we can settle the account.

Carter Ay, and about time.

Vicars climbs down from the cross, and goes off with the Carter

General chatter resumes

Encouraged by Mrs Sydall and other members of the family, everyone is beginning to drift offstage in the direction of the Sydalls' cottage

As the last villagers begin to go, Richard Sydall crosses to Emmot and Rowland who, since the end of the dancing, have not been part of the general celebration, keeping themselves to themselves in obscure corners of the set, or offstage

Richard Sydall Oh, there you are! Come on, Emmot! Everyone will be waiting.

Emmot In a minute, Dad.

Richard Sydall Ah yes, my lass, all right then. Don't be too long though.

Richard Sydall smiles at them and goes, leaving Rowland and Emmot alone on stage

The Lights fade a point or two

Emmot What a noise.

Rowland So many handshakes.

Emmot And kisses.

Rowland Yes . . . How are you?

Emmot All right.

Rowland Really.

Emmot Frightened.

Rowland What?

Emmot A bit.

Rowland Why? The churchyard?

Emmot No, I like it here. It's the only quiet place today.

Rowland Frightened of what, then?

Emmot I don't know. Everything's so brittle.

Rowland Brittle? What's brittle?

Emmot Everything. Me. You.

Rowland Listen, if there's one thing that's not brittle, it's me, I'll tell you that! That's muscle, that is. Solid! All yours that is, come not too many days!

Emmot Too many days, though. So much that can happen.

Rowland Emmot, you're too broody. We'll have none of that when you're my wife, you know, not with the farm to run!

Emmot It's such a strange thing to do, to give yourself to someone else. You can't help being a little bit frightened. Everything's divided by two, whatever you want or think or say becomes double-edged. I haven't got used to it yet.

Rowland You will get used to it. You'll have to, won't you.

Emmot You've got to be so much stronger and cleverer and more careful. It seems unfair.

Rowland Listen, you love me, don't you?

Emmot Aye. I do.

Rowland And I love you, too. So what else do you want?

Emmot I suppose you're right, then, aren't you. To be this minute alive and happy is enough for any one person. Isn't it?

Rowland Course it is. Now come on, we must get back. There's a lot of fellers waiting to get drunk on our behalf tonight.

Emmot Aye, I can tell you the names of some of them, too!

Emmot and Rowland go off together, towards the sound of the celebrations, now quite audible offstage

It is now quite dark as Thomas Stanley enters, alone, in the empty village street

He stops and looks in the direction of the laughing and singing, which continues faintly throughout his scene

Stanley Dear God, how can your sins be justified? This was Paradise, and you gave us a snake. This was Christ, promising life, but we are all dead men, and still waiting. We built you a palace, a clean temple, with the moneytables overturned; but you sent us a whirlwind, and blew it down; and now the marble is fallen, the tombs of the giants lie open to the sky, and our bodies are lifted up for public show. What does a man do, who is left the tenant of a ruin, who is himself a house where the foundations have crumbled, and weeds grow up through the floor? He seizes prayer, and holds to it fast, till his fingers break. Many nights, God, I have met you here, and you have always spoken to me. Now the philistines are back, and the idol-mongers, with their drunkard King and his train of whores. But you have blinded me, taken my tongue, left me for dead, worse . . . I can do nothing, a beggar, going hungry, no man is my friend, and none seem worthy of the love I once gave them for you. Christ in Heaven, your latest humiliation was too much, to break bread with a young boy in the house that was once yours and is now the shelter of your enemies . . .! He has left this place. There is no word now for me. I shall pray still for those few that love him; but my prayers are the prayers of a beggar, my heart is cold, and I know there is no love there. I shall live shadowed, in alleys and corners. Perhaps, if his voice comes again, I shall not be too deaf to hear.

Slowly, Stanley walks off, enclosed in his agony

The Lights lift to mid-morning brightness, and the church bell tolls nine

Francis Frith enters

Francis Frith I took the miser at his word. I was there, first stroke of the bell. But there'll be no sale today.

Richard, Emmot, John, Sarah, Ellen and Mrs Sydall enter in a group

Mrs Sydall (*entering*) If it's George Vicars, it'll all be rubbish, you know that . . .
Richard Sydall Hello, Francis, you've beaten us to it. Haven't you got anything?
Francis Frith I didn't see anything.
Mrs Sydall I wouldn't be surprised if it's all some daft joke, and I've got work to do.
Emmot What's it like, Francis?
Sarah Sydall Are the dresses nice?
John Sydall He says he didn't see.
Ellen Sydall Didn't you like any of it?
Francis Frith The door's bolted. He's ill.

Isaac, Edward, Elizabeth, William, Francis and Mary Thornley enter in a group

Mrs Sydall Ill, is he? Some story that is. He was all right last night.
Isaac Thornley Where's this damn sale, then? Getting me out of bed for a load of rubbish . . .
Richard Sydall It doesn't look like there'll be any sale this morning, Isaac.

Isaac Thornley What do you mean, no sale? I'm back to me bed then . . .

Elizabeth Thornley Wait a minute, Grandad. Why won't there be any sale? You Sydalls got there first, I suppose!

Mrs Sydall Francis was first, if you must know. George is ill, apparently.

Elizabeth Thornley Ill, is he? First I've heard of it!

Mrs Sydall Well, it is only nine o'clock, Mrs Thornley, and you don't hear everything in this village quite as it happens.

Humphrey, Edytha, William, Alice, John, Scythe, Thomas and Frances Torre enter in a group

Richard Sydall All right, then, you're as bad as a couple of hens with your featherpecking.

William Torre What's going on? Where's the sale?

Edward Thornley There's no sale. George is ill.

Humphrey Torre He can't be ill. He's a young man.

Ellen Sydall Well, Francis says he is.

Edward Thornley Just as well, if you ask me. We don't want any fancy clothes from London here.

John Torre What's wrong with him, Francis?

Ellen Sydall Francis has been there.

Francis Frith I don't know. I banged on the door, but Mrs Cooper told me to go away because he'd been ill all night.

Mrs Sydall Isn't it terrible, Mrs Thornley, not knowing?

Elizabeth Thornley Very annoying. We must go and have a word with Mrs Cooper.

Unwin and Merril enter

Unwin All right, all right, you can stop all your questions, *I* can tell you the whole story . . .

Merril Just as *I* heard it, direct from the widow Cooper's own mouth . . .

Unwin Shortly after she told me. Last night, you see, while we were all enjoying ourselves, George opened up his black box from London . . .

Merril And there they were! Golds and silvers, silks and taffetas, all shining in the candlelight!

Unwin But when he feels them a bit, he finds they're a bit damp from the journey, so what does he do?

Merril He hangs them up on a rail in front of the fire to dry . . .

Unwin And within ten minutes . . .

Merril Nearer five if you ask me . . .

Unwin I didn't, so shut up.

Merril Nearer five . . .

Unwin He complained of a headache,

Merril And a queasy feeling . . .

Unwin So the widow Cooper packed him straight to bed,

Merril Where he was sick all night, all over her best sheets.

Unwin Twisting and screaming like a slit pig.

Merril And he's no better this morning!
Unwin Possibly worse!

Chatter and discussion break out at a high pitch

Mompesson enters

Mompesson What's the matter?

The chatter ceases, but no-one answers. There is still a strong antipathy

   Is anything wrong?
Edward Thornley George Vicars is ill.
Mompesson Oh. What's wrong with him?
Edward Thornley If we knew that, we'd be helping him, not talking about it.
Mompesson You'd better send for the doctor.
Edward Thornley There's no doctor. You're the doctor here.
Mompesson Me? But I know nothing about it . . .
Edward Thornley You're supposed to be the rector, aren't you?
Mompesson I know my duty, Mr Thornley.
Edward Thornley Ah. Pity you don't know your parishioners as well!
Mompesson I know very well, Mr Thornley, what you and some others here think of me. Since you seem determined to hate me, there is nothing I can do but pray for you.
Edward Thornley And George Vicars can go hang, and us with him!
Mompesson I am a man of God, sir, not a doctor. (*He turns to go*)

Jonathan Cooper enters up C, *and calls to Mompesson*

Jonathan Cooper You must come to my mother's cottage, Rector . . .
Mompesson I can do nothing but pray for him, Mr Cooper, I haven't the skill . . .
Jonathan Cooper That's it, sir. He keeps asking for you. My mother would have come herself, but he keeps being sick, and saying wild things, and she can't leave him.
Richard Sydall What's wrong with him, Jon?
Jonathan Cooper A fever and vomiting, and his tongue like a dry black leather, and a red rash like roses on his skin. Please come, Rector, my mother says he may be dying.

A burst of excited and concerned chatter from the crowd. Mompesson seems unsure of himself, uncertain what to do or what is expected of him

Mompesson Yes—yes.

Mompesson seems to decide suddenly, and moves quickly upstage, Cooper following. The others prepare to follow in a crowd. Up to this point Mompesson has always been shy and retiring with the villagers, but now he turns, and calls to them in a voice of firmness and strength

   No. Stop!

The crowd silences. Mompesson's voice assumes its normal diffidence

One man is ill. If he is in pain, he has no wish to become a public spectacle. I shall speak to him and to God, and if it is his will, he will soon be recovered. We all have work to do. Go and do yours.

Mompesson looks at them for a moment and then exits up C *with Jonathan Cooper. All the villagers exit talking quietly, with the exception of Richard and Mrs Sydall, and Edward and Elizabeth Thornley*

Edward Thornley There's your new rector, Sydall. He has to be driven to visit a sick man.

Elizabeth Thornley Mr Stanley never had to be sent for.

Richard Sydall Don't be unjust, Edward. He doesn't know us yet, or our ways.

Edward Thornley I'll give him six weeks. And I tell you, Richard, at the end of that time we'll be glad to drive him out with staves.

Richard Sydall Well. You may be right. But a lot can happen in six weeks.

Edward Thornley I hope so, for his sake.

Richard Sydall And ours.

Richard and Mrs Sydall and Edward and Elizabeth Thornley exit together L

The Lights centre on the cottage area up R, *which opens to reveal the interior of Mrs Cooper's cottage. George Vicars is in bed, Mrs Cooper beside him. Edward Cooper sits in a chair facing downstage, with his head in his hands. The black box is seen, standing open, and a rail, on which some of the clothes are hanging*

Jonathan Cooper and Mompesson enter from a door at the back

Mrs Cooper Thank the Lord you've come, Rector, I don't know what to do any more.

Mompesson How is he?

Mrs Cooper Quiet all of a sudden. But all night he's been screaming and crying and sick. I've tried everything, Rector, but I've never seen anything like this before.

Mompesson I know nothing about sick people I'm afraid, Mrs Cooper . . .

Mrs Cooper Look at his neck.

Mompesson Where?

Mrs Cooper That patch was red early this morning. It went black and hard suddenly. There's one twice the size on his chest, and more under his arms and between his toes. He's been bringing up blood and sick all night.

Vicars Is that you, Rector? I can't see.

Mompesson I'm here, and with me is God to comfort you.

Vicars I can't see.

Mrs Cooper You'll get no sense out of him, Rector. He's been talking all night, but nothing to understand.

Vicars Who's that coming through the door?

Mompesson There's no-one.

Vicars Yes, there is. The lining stinks of blood, his face has gone rotten . . .! Give me some water, please . . .!

Mompesson kneels and begins to say the prayer for the dying, a mumble, but just audible. Mrs Cooper comes downstage to her son Edward, still sitting in the chair. As she does so Edward sneezes violently, and stands up, still holding his head with one hand

Mrs Cooper Edward?

Edward Cooper Can you get rid of the flowers, Mother. They're making me sneeze.

Mrs Cooper There are no flowers, son. I've had none in since the day before yesterday.

Edward Cooper Fruit then. That's it. Rotten apples. Some of the apples in the tub must have gone bad.

Mrs Cooper What are you talking about, son?

Edward Cooper Something sweet. Can't you smell it?

Mrs Cooper Oh, don't fuss, I can't smell anything.

Edward Cooper You must have a cold, then.

Mrs Cooper Will you go down the well again for me? He's drunk the last bucketful.

Edward Cooper Yes, all right. Oh! My head feels like the anvil.

Mrs Cooper I'm not surprised, the night we had of it. You can have a nice lie down when you've got me the water.

Edward Cooper Yes, I think I will.

Edward Cooper exits with the bucket

Mompesson rises and rejoins Mrs Cooper. Jonathan Cooper stays by the bed

Mrs Cooper How is he now?

Mompesson Quiet again. I don't think he could hear me.

Mrs Cooper Poor man.

Mompesson When did he get like this?

Mrs Cooper Well, it was like this, you see. He unpacked his box, straight after he'd paid off the carter it was, just after I'd given him some dinner, and he put the things to air in front of the fire. Then, when he came back from the wake, he had another good look at them. Then about midnight he said he wasn't well.

Mompesson Is that the box?

Mrs Cooper Ay, that's it.

Mompesson And those are the clothes? (*He turns them over with his hands*)

Mrs Cooper Ay, lovely they are, a friend of his bought them for him in London, and had them sent down here. He said they'd make his fortune.

Mompesson suddenly draws his hands away, as though stung, and stands dead still. He seems on the point of running in panic from the room, but manages to control himself, and becomes precise

Mompesson From London, you say.
Mrs Cooper That's right.
Mompesson You're quite sure?
Mrs Cooper Ay, his friend's a draper in Thames Street.
Mompesson And he bought them—recently?
Mrs Cooper Ay, I think so. He told me about it a couple of months ago, I think. Why?
Mompesson For—er—no particular reason.

Jonathan Cooper stands up behind them

Jonathan Cooper Rector.
Mompesson Yes?
Jonathan Cooper He's dead.

Mompesson goes quickly to the bed, and Mrs Cooper follows. Mompesson lifts his eyelids, stands back and bows his head

Mompesson Lord have mercy on us.
Jonathan Cooper Christ have mercy on us.
Mrs Cooper Christ have mercy on us.

They stand for a moment, heads bowed in prayer. Then Mompesson lifts the sheet and looks at the dead man's chest. He comes away from the bed and beckons to the other two

Mompesson Listen to me.
Jonathan Cooper What is it, Rector?
Mompesson I don't want you to touch him at all.
Mrs Cooper What did he die of, Rector?
Mompesson Wrap him in the sheet he's lying in, and sew it up. I'll send the undertaker round straight away.
Jonathan Cooper Straight away?
Mompesson I want to get him buried this afternoon. Scour the box out with soap, and burn all those clothes.
Mrs Cooper Burn them?
Mompesson And scour the box. And don't tell anyone about it.
Jonathan Cooper But they already know, you saw.
Mompesson His face I mean, what he looks like. There's no point in frightening people.
Mrs Cooper He does look bad, with them blotches and scabs.
Jonathan Cooper We won't say anything.
Mompesson I must go now. Don't try to wash him.
Mrs Cooper Poor man, Rector, he can't be buried dirty . . .
Mompesson I'm afraid he must be. Sew him up, and burn those things. I'll find the carpenter and be back as soon as I can.

Mompesson exits through the door at the back

Mrs Cooper I can't believe it, Jon. Last night he was well.

Jonathan Cooper Fifteen hours ago. Not a day. I wonder why we mustn't tell anybody?

Mrs Cooper Never mind why if the rector says so. We'd better get started.

Edward Cooper (*off*) Mother!

Mrs Cooper What is it, son?

Edward Cooper (*off*) Can you bring me a cup for the water?

Mrs Cooper Don't shout, Edward! With poor George lying dead in here!

Edward Cooper comes and stands in the doorway looking

I do hope your eldest son's not as lazy as mine!

Mrs Cooper goes busily off. Edward looks at Vicars from the doorway, rubs his forehead, and goes off

Jonathan Cooper crosses to Vicars, lifts the sheet and looks at his face

Jonathan Cooper It's like a ring of roses . . .

The Lights fade on the cottage area, and come up on the rectory area, at night. Catherine sits reading by candlelight. Mompesson is too tense and disturbed to concentrate. There is a tension building between them which has to find expression. Catherine is aware of it, but waits patiently for him to speak

Mompesson Catherine!

She looks up

I have something to tell you.

Catherine What?

Mompesson I am unworthy of this calling. I have no love for these people. None. Only disgust. At the death bed and at the funeral I tasted vomit in my mouth.

Catherine The first death . . .

Mompesson And of course, they want Stanley, not me. I read a plain text in all their faces. Rejection. I have nothing to offer them, and they know it.

Catherine Don't lie to yourself, William, or to me.

Mompesson I'm not lying. Am I lying?

Catherine I know how much strength is in you. Are you afraid of it? Must you keep it in chains, like a monster away from the light?

Mompesson No, no, it isn't true, I wish it were. Such weapons as I have are mental ones, and they are useless here—I shall write and resign the living.

Catherine And will you run away from every place, as you are running now?

Mompesson Running? I wish it were so simple. There is nothing here to run from.

Catherine There are three hundred and fifty people, and they are your responsibility. They can spit in your eye and beat you with staves, but they can't change that.

An agonized pause as Mompesson recognizes one of his true motives

Mompesson There is something else.
Catherine What?
Mompesson George Vicars: when he died.
Catherine Yes?
Mompesson I saw his face. And the marks.
Catherine Marks?
Mompesson Marks on his skin. I think I've seen them before. I think I know what they are.

There is a loud banging on their door, and a voice shouting "Rector". They look at each other for a moment as the banging continues

Open it.

Catherine looks at him, and goes to the door

Mrs Cooper enters

Catherine Mrs Cooper . . .

Mrs Cooper moves directly to Mompesson, and looks at him, saying nothing

Mompesson What is it, Mrs Cooper?
Mrs Cooper You were there, weren't you, Rector.
Mompesson What?
Mrs Cooper At my cottage this morning.
Mompesson Yes.
Mrs Cooper Not twelve hours ago.
Mompesson Yes.
Mrs Cooper You saw my son Edward.

Mompesson is silent

He had a headache, didn't he.
Mompesson Yes. I believe so.
Mrs Cooper He can't be dead, can he?

Silence

God bless me, sir, he's lying there white as a lily, with a ring of roses on his cheek

Catherine sits her down, then speaks so that Mrs Cooper cannot hear her

Catherine What is it, William?
Mompesson (*unemotionally*) I think it's plague.
Mrs Cooper White as a lily and dead as a stone.

Mompesson walks away from Mrs Cooper, beckoning Catherine to him

Catherine What shall we do?

Mompesson Try to calm Mrs Cooper first of all. It will be better if the villagers don't know.

Catherine They're sure to find out.

Mompesson But not at once. We will have some time to think how to stop it.

Catherine How do you stop the plague?

Mompesson I don't know.

Catherine They dug pits for the bodies in London. There were so many.

Mompesson But here there are only two. We have no need of pits and gravecarts for them.

Catherine crosses over to the still weeping Mrs Cooper, and gently ushers her off

Mompesson follows and watches. He then returns to the middle of the stage, looking off in the direction of the cross, and rubbing his face with indecision

Mompesson No. I mustn't be foolish. Two dead men are nothing.

Mompesson strides off after Catherine, as—

the CURTAIN *falls*

ACT II

As the CURTAIN *rises, the church bell is tolling slowly, and the stage is empty*

Over this sound we hear a cackle and hooting of laughter, and the tinkle of the Bedlam's bell. He enters L, *still hooting and cackling, and bouncing up and down on his bent legs*

Bedlam I seen it, I seen it! (*He whispers, as though a secret*) Three new graves, open in the churchyard. I laughed and danced, but they sent me away. They don't think it's funny: putting a man in a hole.

Four villagers enter up C, *hooded in black, carrying a coffin. They make slowly down* L

Bedlam stands down C *with his back to the audience, and turns his head*

They've got Peter Halksworth in that long box.

He walks over and looks. The bearers take no notice

They've nailed him in. In case he changes his mind.

A second similar cortège enters up R, *followed by a third down* R, *both crossing down* L

The Bedlam dances over, weaving between them

They've put Thomas Thorpe in that one, because he didn't wake up this morning when they shook him. And in that one his wife Mary. Just because her toes went black. They owned a shop. But last night a white cricket sang at the back door, and this morning the shutters are closed.

The corteges exit. As the last goes off, the bell stops

They've stopped all the music, and planted them in the earth. Perhaps they think they'll grow, like flowers.

Mompesson enters briskly down L, *walking up* C

Bedlam Mister!
Mompesson I'm sorry, boy, I'm in a hurry . . .

Bedlam Can I come with you?

Mompesson Not now, I must see Mrs Sydall's daughter.

Bedlam I been playing in the grass by the church.

Mompesson I know, you mustn't play there.

Bedlam I seen four graves.

Mompesson Three you mean.

Bedlam No, four. There's one all grass, not open yet.

Mompesson looks at him curiously for a moment, then becomes brisk again

Mompesson There's no time now, boy. Tell me your dreams another day.

Mompesson exits up C

Bedlam shouts after him, his words gradually becoming terrified

Bedlam And I seen another one, and another, and another, all in a line, and black buds on all the trees, and a forest of crosses growing up the street, and over the river and all across the valley, till it's all thick and dark, no more people, just big black trees . . . !

He is alone on stage

Nobody listens to the madboy.

The Bedlam runs off, his bell tinkling

The Lights cross-fade to the cottage area up R *and we see a tableau. The only furniture is a bed. On it lies Sarah Sydall. By the bed Stanley kneels in prayer. Mrs Sydall, Richard, Ellen and Emmot stand with their backs to the audience. There is a knock at the door. Richard Sydall opens it. No-one else moves*

Mompesson enters

Mompesson I'm sorry to be so long, I was delayed at the . . . (*He stops as he sees the girl*)

Stanley rises from his knees and covers her with the sheet. He then turns to Mompesson

When did she die?

Richard Sydall Ten minutes ago. She got ill during the night.

Stanley I'm sorry, sir, to have had to kneel in your place. But the prayer of an exile is better than no prayer at all. God's blessing to all here.

Richard Sydall Amen.

All Sydalls Amen.

Mrs Sydall Thank you, Mr Stanley.

Stanley exits through the cottage door

Mompesson I'm sorry I was not here . . .

Richard Sydall We have enough sorrow of our own, Rector. We don't need yours.

Mompesson I will make it my business to see the carpenter and make the necessary arrangements.

Richard Sydall Too late again, Rector. My son John is there now.

Mompesson Then there is nothing more I can do.

Richard Sydall No sir, nothing.

Pause, as Richard looks at him

Mompesson Don't look at me like Judas, Mr Sydall. My business was at the Thorpes', and as sadly urgent as yours.

Richard Sydall Tom Thorpe died last night.

Mompesson And so did Mary this morning.

Mrs Sydall No, not Mary . . .

Mompesson There were two children left alone.

Mrs Sydall Are they all right?

Mompesson My wife is with them. Tell me, did she, Sarah, did she go out last night?

Mrs Sydall Only to Mrs Cooper's yesterday afternoon, to take a parcel for me.

Mompesson Oh. I see.

Mrs Sydall Why is it, Rector? What sin have we committed?

Mompesson God—has his reasons.

Richard Sydall For six people, in a few days, like this? My Sarah didn't know the meaning of wrongdoing. And look at her child's face, covered in filthy black scabs!

Mompesson God's mercy to this stricken house.

Richard Sydall Aye. He ignored our prayers last night, so perhaps he'll listen to us this morning.

Mompesson looks at them for a moment and then goes out into the street

The Lights cross-fade, leaving the cottage in darkness. Stanley is sitting on the pedestal of the cross with a Bible in his hands, reading. Mompesson sees him. Then walks past him down L. Then stops, and turns

Mompesson Mr Stanley.

Stanley puts away his book, looks up and says nothing

I'd like to talk to you.

Stanley There's nothing to say, sir. You were not there, and I took your place, for which I have apologized.

Mompesson No, no, not that. We are both servants of the same God . . .

Stanley Untrue, sir. I have spent my life fighting against everything you stand for. I have been beaten but I have not been humiliated, nor have I betrayed myself.

Mompesson Mr Stanley . . .

Stanley Talking to you is unfair, Mompesson. It opens wounds in my side which you are too young to know about. It's better to keep silent. Good afternoon.

Stanley begins to go down R. *Mompesson is at a loss. Stanley is just leaving when he calls*

Mompesson You know what it is, don't you!

Stanley stops dead then turns

Stanley Yes, I know what it is.
Mompesson You know what the black scabs mean.
Stanley Plague.
Mompesson They had it in London this year, people were dying a thousand a week.
Stanley Yes.
Mompesson What are we going to do?
Stanley What do you mean?
Mompesson We must make some plan together.
Stanley You may do as you please. I shall do nothing.
Mompesson Nothing? You must help me, Stanley, or more people will die.
Stanley Do you know nothing at all but what you have read in books? When God sends the plague into a house the Angel of Death takes residence. When he leaves, he leaves a tomb. Do you understand?
Mompesson Is there no cure?
Stanley You can lance the boils when they first appear; you can make them drink hot water. If the boils turn black, the best thing you can do is to take a spade and start digging.
Mompesson Is that all?
Stanley I have told you all I know. You are the rector now. You won't want advice from an outlaw and a beggar.
Mompesson There are houses here where even death won't make me welcome . . . It isn't long since these were your people. They haven't changed.
Stanley But I have, and now they are yours. You must do as you choose.
Mompesson I choose to ask your help . . . I'm a stranger here, a young man, and I find it hard—to make myself loved. You are older—perhaps wiser than I am . . . Don't look at me like that, Stanley, people are dying who might have lived, and all I ask is your counsel . . .
Stanley Listen to me, Mompesson, you are not my judge passing sentence . . .
Mompesson That was never in my mind . . .
Stanley I gave these people fifteen years of service; every morsel of my precious God they had at my hands, I gave my love, and they took it and returned no thanks. There is none left now, sir, I am empty. When the King returned there was more than one loyal cheer, and many prayers of thanksgiving. Seeing that has blinded me—I gave them the hard discipline of God's service . . .

Mompesson They need now his mercy.

Stanley Let them seek it on their knees then.

Mompesson Is there nothing we can do together? I have been called for in three houses already this morning, and the day isn't ended yet. I shall need all one man's strength.

Stanley "As thy days, so shall thy strength be."

Mompesson Is that all you can offer?

Stanley Do you expect riches from a beggar? (*He walks towards the exit, then stops and turns*) If you tell them to stay in their houses, you will have done all you can do.

Mompesson I shall pray for them, Stanley. I shall pray till my heart bursts!

Stanley Yes, pray. I prayed when my hour came, but my prayer wasn't answered. This hour is yours.

Stanley exits R. *Catherine enters* L

Catherine Where have you been?

Mompesson At the Sydalls'. Their daughter is dead.

Catherine The same way?

Mompesson Yes. What about the Thorpe children?

Catherine I persuaded their aunt to take them in. She looked at them as though they were lepers. I'm tired now.

Mompesson Soon the villagers will know. Every door will be bolted then.

Catherine What are we going to do? It may be us next.

Mompesson You mustn't say that.

Catherine Don't be frightened for me. They say the plague only takes the strong.

Mompesson You must keep away from the infected houses.

Catherine My place is where you are. If you must be there, I must be with you.

Mompesson I feel so helpless. As though a great wheel has started to roll, and I am left watching. Nothing is as I planned it. Three days ago I thought it best to leave here.

Catherine And now?

Mompesson I saw it so clearly, but it wasn't this. I was to be the great preacher, with a tongue like a whip! But these are good people, their worst sin a missed service on Sunday, or a day late in bed. My weapons are useless, and my insufficiency is left naked. Now I must be their father, and I don't know how to begin.

Catherine With love. They will need love.

Mompesson Many of them hate me. Catherine, I haven't the words to do it . . .

Catherine Love doesn't need words.

Mompesson I shall *make* them love me, I shall *make* them. Even if I must kiss their black sores to do it. Stanley thinks I will crumble, but if God wants me here, I shall stay at his bidding.

Catherine You may not be loved yet, but already you are needed.

Mompesson But I wanted to fight. Here there is no enemy I can see.
Catherine There may be no enemy, but there is a battle for sure. Are you
running, or do you stand?
Mompesson I stand.

Mompesson and Catherine exit L

The church bell begins to toll slowly

*A large crowd of villagers begins to appear. All the Hancocks, Friths,
Thornleys, John and Deborah Wilson, Elizabeth Swanne, Lydia Chapman, Rowland and George Mower, Howe, Unwin and Merril.*

*The bell continues, and they all group themselves round the mid-stage L
rostra, as if watching a funeral off L. The bell ceases*

*Almost at once the Torres begin to enter, all except Scythe, who is dead.
They have black cloaks over their dresses. Edytha and Humphrey are
first, followed by Frances, John and Thomas, and finally William and
Alice. As they appear, the crowd stumbles and shuffles away leaving a
clear way to the exit. The Torres stop and gather in a group round William,
the tallest. The younger ones are frightened. There is silence for a moment*

Edward Thornley Pass on to your house, William Torre, and stay there.
William Torre Why do you draw back?
Edward Thornley The earth's still soft on your son's coffin.
William Torre You were my friends yesterday. Now the streets are empty
when I pass.
Edward Thornley We want to stay alive.
William Torre Will I kill you?

He moves towards them, hands outstretched. They all stumble away

Yesterday my son was living. Two weeks ago you were dancing to his
pipes at the wake. God's hand came into my house with no warning
and took my son. For all your drawing back, it can come as easily
into yours. What happens then? Will all neighbours be strangers?

There is no reaction. He shouts

Draw back then now. Your turn will come!
Edytha Torre Come home, son. Leave them.

*All the Torres begin to go together. Just before they exit, William shouts
again, in a terrible, grief-stricken voice*

William Torre Your turn will come!

The Torres exit

*The crowd begins to disperse. Edward Thornley jumps on to the pedestal of
the cross and shouts to them*

Edward Thornley Don't go, listen to me!

The crowd ceases its murmur and listens

Something terrible is happening in our village. One month ago, George Vicars died, with black scabs on his face and chest. Since then ten more people have died the same way, the last today. Now, are we blind, or children, or what?

William Hancock What can we do? People are dying and nobody knows why.

Francis Frith The Rector told Mrs Cooper it's a strange fever from Africa.

Edward Thornley You may believe that if you like. But I'll tell you what I think.

Howe Listen to the oracle!

A burst of laughter from the villagers. Edward Thornley shouts above it

Edward Thornley It's the plague!

The laughter ceases. There is a moment's silence. Then a frightened chatter begins as people start to move off in all directions

Don't run away like sheep when the dog barks! Listen to me if you want to stay alive!

Elizabeth Frith If it's the plague we can't do anything.

Mrs Hancock How do you get it?

John Wilson It's a clammy invisible mist in the air.

George Frith You take it in with your breath. You can't do anything about it.

Frances Frith You must carry flowers pinned to your breast. The sweet smell drives it away.

Mrs Hancock Is that what they do in London?

John Hancock In London they run away to the country!

Edward Thornley If we panic like this we are all dead men.

George Frith What can we do?

Mrs Hancock We can't do anything, oh God, save us all!

Edward Thornley We can act like reasonable Christian men. We can pray to God, and we can take care.

John Wilson What do you mean?

Edward Thornley No-one must go near the infected houses, nor touch, nor speak to, nor even look at anyone from them. We must shut ourselves inside our own families till the danger is over.

George Frith How can we? There's work to be done.

Edward Thornley Do you want to live? It may be your parents, or your own wife and child. If you want to live you must avoid them all like lepers. The dead must be buried by nearest kin, no stranger must see them.

William Hancock That's sacrilege, Edward Thornley.

Edward Thornley Is it sacrilege to shield your neighbour? If we don't, it will be all over the village within a month, and we won't be able to stop it. But if we act now, before it can get a hold——

Unwin You won't stop it that way.

Edward Thornley If you've nothing better to say, old man, you can keep quiet.

Unwin I've plenty to say. I've seen it all before.

George Frith You've seen it?

Unwin Old men have long memories. You remember it, Isaac Thornley, and you, Andrew Merril. Curbar in thirty-two!

Isaac Thornley Ah, before the war.

Merril A lot of people died there that autumn.

Unwin Nearly fifty of them.

George Frith Fifty!

Edward Thornley Now do you believe me? Go home, and keep yourselves to yourselves.

The crowd begins to disperse during the next section, till Howe, Unwin, Merril and Isaac Thornley are left alone

Unwin Do you remember Frank Rowley, Merril?

Isaac Thornley He were a big man.

Merril Ay. Bigger than you, Marshall Howe.

Howe What happened to him?

As Unwin begins to tell the story, groups of villagers listen to parts of it, and then leave, frightened by what they have heard

Unwin There were eight in that family. Over in Curbar it was, not ten miles away. There was him and his father and mother.

Merril And his wife and four children, wasn't it?

Unwin His wife got it first.

Merril Then his father and his two sons, and then his mother. All of them dead inside a week.

Unwin He had to bury them with his own hands, no-one else would come near them.

Merril He dragged them to their graves in a field, feet first, with a bit of rope.

Unwin Till there was only him left, and his twin little girls. Six years old they were.

Howe And did they survive?

Unwin Survive? You're as bad as young Thornley you are.

Merril The plague's a glutton. It keeps eating till it goes bust.

Unwin The morning after his mother died, he felt ill, hot and thirsty, with a headache.

Merril Frank Rowley were a big man, Marshall Howe. Bigger than you are.

Isaac Thornley Too big for six-year-olds to carry.

Merril Aye.

Unwin So he went again to the field where his family lay sleeping, and he took his spade and some straw, and he dug his sixth grave that week.

And when he'd finished, he lined it with straw. The bed must be comfortable that's going to hold you forever.

Merril Then he laid himself down on the straw in the hole, and waited for God to release him.

Unwin He waited all that day, and all night in his delirium.

Isaac Thornley He were a big man, you see.

Unwin And when he saw the sun rise on the next day, he closed his eyes and died.

Howe And the two children?

Merril Died a few days later.

Unwin And were left for the crows to peck at.

Howe And it's here now, like a hawk above the village, waiting to swoop.

Unwin And I'll tell you why all those people died.

Howe Do I need telling?

Unwin They died because they were weak and afraid. Because they were all waiting to die, and as soon as they got a headache they gave up, that's why! You need willpower—(*he taps his head*)—in here. Like I've got!

Merril You're talking rubbish, Unwin.

Isaac Thornley You had the clap when you were a lad, I remember.

Unwin I've had everything I have, plague, smallpox, and the big pox, too, I've had the lot!

Merril Ay, more than once, too.

Unwin I'll tell you something, Marshall Howe, and you, Merril.

Howe Tell me, Solomon.

Unwin When you wake up one morning and your head's aching and your tongue's like a dry washleather, you say to yourself, "I've got a headache, and I need a drink", no more. And you'll live out all the days God sends, mark my words.

Howe I'll remember that.

Rowland Torre enters and makes his way across the stage towards the cottage area

Merril Where do you think you're going, Rowland Torre?

Rowland A carrier came to our farm this morning, and he brought bad news.

Merril Oh ah. He would.

Rowland Is it true, then?

Unwin Bad news always is.

Rowland About Sarah?

Howe You're out of date. That was a week ago.

Unwin Six more are dead since then.

Rowland What? What about Emmot? Is Emmot all right?

Unwin Don't ask us, boy. Nobody's been near that house for a week. I wouldn't give you much for her chances.

Merril Nor any of that family.

Howe Nor you, if you go there.

Rowland I must go.
Howe Don't be a fool, Rowland. There's a long life waiting for you at home.

But Rowland ignores them and moves quickly off

Merril Come back, madman!
Howe You might just as well dam the sea.
Unwin So much for young Thornley. I told him what his taking care would come to.
Merril He'll take it back to Middleton, that's what he'll do.
Unwin People are like rivers. As long as the moon shines they will flow together. Nothing can stop them.
Howe Well. We can only wait now.
Unwin And see who goes next.

Unwin grins at Merril, and they all go off in opposite directions

Cross-fade to the cottage area, where Richard Sydall is standing by the fire, wrapped in a blanket

Rowland enters

Richard Sydall turns to him

Richard Sydall Go away.
Rowland It's me, Mr Sydall.
Richard Sydall I said go away.
Rowland I came to say how sorry I am about . . .
Richard Sydall Yes, thank you, now go.
Rowland Where's Emmot?
Richard Sydall She's in there.
Rowland Is she all right?
Richard (*shouting*) Yes, she's all right, now go!
Rowland I want to see her.
Richard Sydall You can't see her today.
Rowland Why? Are you all right, you're shivering.
Richard Sydall Are you blind, boy? Don't come near me!

Rowland stops, horrified

I've got the plague. Get out of here!
Rowland I'm not frightened.
Richard Sydall You may be frightened or not, son. But I've got a boil coming here on my cheek. It will go hard soon, and then black. By tomorrow I shall be dead.
Rowland Don't say that! Look, I'm sure you'll be better soon . . .
Richard Sydall Go away and leave me in peace! There's a good lad. I want to die like a man, not like a child.

Rowland You don't look too bad . . .

Richard Sydall You fool! I've been sitting here all morning turning myself to stone. Now you come, sturdy as a tree, and tell me I'll be all right . . . Go away! (*He begins to cry, trying hard not to*)

Rowland I'm sorry.

Mrs Sydall enters and crouches down beside her husband, holding him

Mrs Sydall Haven't you seen enough yet? Go away.

Rowland turns and is going, when Emmot's voice is heard calling off. He stops and turns

Emmot (*off*) Rowland, can you hear me?

Rowland Yes, Emmot, I can hear you.

Emmot (*off*) I can't come in to see you. I must stay in here with John and Ellen and the twins till Father is better.

Rowland Yes.

Emmot (*off*) You mustn't come here again, Rowland.

Rowland What? Emmot, I must see you!

Emmot (*off*) The door will be bolted.

Rowland I can see you at the window. We can talk through the shutters.

Emmot (*off*) No, you can't. I want you to, Rowland, but it's too dangerous.

Rowland When will I see you again?

Emmot (*off*) I don't know. I don't know.

Rowland It's no good, Emmot,· danger or not, I'll break the door down!

Emmot (*off*) Rowland, please . . .

Rowland What?

Emmot (*off*) If you promise you won't come back, I'll see you on Sunday afternoon. On the slope above Cussy Dell, you know it there?

Rowland I know it, yes.

Emmot (*off*) Promise me, Rowland, you won't come back into the village!

Rowland All right, Emmot, I promise . . .

Emmot (*off*) I'll see you on Sunday. God willing.

Rowland Emmot! Emmot! (*He bangs the door again*)

Mrs Sydall Must she burst her heart with crying before you'll go?

Rowland God be with you, then.

Mrs Sydall Ay. We have need of him here.

Rowland moves to the door. As he gets there Richard Sydall begins to groan in agony. Mrs Sydall cuddles him and whispers words of comfort which we do not hear. Rowland is watching. She looks at him, and he sees for the first time that she is streaming tears

(*Sobbing*) Go away.

Rowland goes out of the door and off

The Lights dim out in the cottage area and come up on the main area. music is heard. The Lights become hard and brilliant

The Bedlam enters, turning in circles, and holding up his hands, as though catching snowflakes

Bedlam Snow—snow—snow—I'm going to build a snowman for Christmas. I'll make him big and strong, like Marshall Howe, with a hat and a clay pipe, and a stick in his hand. He'll be all right while it stays freezing. But when it gets warmer, his face will go black and dirty, and he'll get old, and when the sun comes out again, I'll watch him melt away to a little pool of dirty water. Then he'll be all gone, and there'll be nothing left except his hat and his clay pipe and his stick, and I expect I'll wonder why I bothered to make him at all. (*He looks very sad for a second. Then he bends down, scrabbling in the snow and making noises*)

Rowland Torre enters

Hallo, mister. I'm going to build a snowman.
Rowland What are you doing up here? You'll get cold in those rags.
Bedlam I don't feel the cold. Are you going to help me?
Rowland Not today. I'm waiting for someone. Go back and play in the village.
Bedlam I seen you here before.
Rowland Yes.
Bedlam Every Sunday, in the afternoon. For a long time.
Rowland Six weeks.
Bedlam I don't like it in the village now.
Rowland Why?
Bedlam Everybody keeps crying. And they shoo me away when I dance.
Rowland Has anyone else died?
Bedlam Buzzz, buz, buzzzzz.
Rowland Do you understand? Have more people been dying?
Bedlam Can I have your hat for my snowman?
Rowland Do you know Emmot Sydall?
Bedlam I don't understand names.
Rowland You know the cottage, nearly opposite the church gate . . . ?
Bedlam They make boxes in that house.
Rowland Boxes?
Bedlam They make a box, and then they take it as a present for the black-man in the church. Then they go back and make another one. I seen them.
Rowland Listen carefully, boy. Tell me, which one have you seen?
Bedlam I don't understand names.

Emmot appears up C. She is white faced and ill looking, and her clothes are beginning to look ragged and uncared for. Throughout this scene she speaks as though very tired

Emmot Rowland . . .

Rowland Emmot . . .! All right, boy, go and build your snowman. Here's a penny for you.

Bedlam I haven't had a penny for a long time. I'd throw it in the brook and watch it roll, but it's frozen up.

The Bedlam runs off

Rowland Emmot, are you all right . . .? (*He makes to go to her*)

Emmot No, don't come near me! Stay where you are and we can talk.

Rowland You are all right, aren't you? You look so . . .

Emmot Don't worry, Rowland, I haven't had the plague yet.

Rowland Don't say it like that, Emmot. You'll be all right now the winter's come. It's too cold.

Emmot I suppose it must be winter now.

Rowland It's nearly Christmas!

Emmot Christmas . . .

Rowland We killed the geese yesterday, and there'll be fruit and cakes and puddings. You must bring up your whole family.

Emmot My family . . .?

Rowland Emmot . . .?

Emmot I said I'd come and see you that Sunday.

Rowland I came every week.

Emmot I saw you across the Dell.

Rowland Why didn't you come?

She lowers her head

Tell me, Emmot. (*He moves towards her*)

Emmot No, stay where you are!

She looks up, and the expression on her face stops him dead in his tracks

Father died on the Sunday night. The day after you came. Mother made us stay in the other room, and we heard him crying. It's an indescribable noise, Rowland, a grown man dying: like a baby sobbing, except that it's low and deep. Mother wouldn't let us see him. The carpenter left a coffin outside the door, but he wouldn't come in. My mother had to do it all herself, even the nails. We stayed in during the week after the funeral, and it seemed all right. I was going to come and see you when I promised. Then on Saturday night, John got ill—my little brother John, and on Sunday morning Ellen was ill, too. John died at dinnertime on Sunday, and Ellen on Monday morning. I saw it all that time. My mother couldn't manage two by herself. She kept crying and saying, "I'm sorry, Emmot, but you've got to help me with them". We stayed in the next week, too. There were other people dying in the village. Some of your cousins Torre, I think, but I don't know who. We just saw the coffins going past the window. The next Saturday —a week to the day, both the baby twins got ill. Only two, they didn't have any idea what was happening, except that it hurt. Elizabeth died on the Sunday. It seemed as though Alice was getting better, but on

Tuesday night she died, too. Then there was just my mother and me. Every day we sat opposite each other at the table, always on the same chairs, waiting for the first sign which of us would be the next. Which would have to bury the other. We've been sitting like that for three weeks. But nothing has happened. Others are dying, but we pray that God has finished with us. We've been in the house all that time. Today is the first time I've been out since Alice was buried. We've been sitting there, all day, every day, listening to the church bell. It's a month since Alice died now, and it seemed as safe as it ever will be. So I came. That's why I haven't been before, Rowland.

There is nothing Rowland can say. They are still at a distance. Agonized, he makes a swift movement to her, and embraces her before she can object. She struggles

Rowland, no, you mustn't . . .
Rowland Who says I mustn't . . .
Emmot I've been living with the plague for two months, it must be all over me, in my clothes and hair . . .

He kisses her on the mouth. She struggles for a moment, then relaxes

Rowland There. If anything happens now, it happens to both of us.
Emmot You shouldn't have done that, Rowland.
Rowland Shhhhhh . . .

He kisses her again

Come away with me, Emmot, back to the farm where it's safe.
Emmot No. (*She breaks a little away from him*)
Rowland No? Why not . . .?
Emmot I can't leave my mother alone . . . Anyway, they say in the village the cold weather will end it all.
Rowland Why take the risk? Come with me.
Emmot I can't, Rowland. I might bring it with me.
Rowland Does that matter, if we're together?
Emmot Your family might think so.
Rowland They'll welcome you.
Emmot No, Rowland, I must stay with my mother. Then perhaps, when it's safe . . . The rector will look after us. I think he and his wife must be saints. They've been to every house that's been visited, every day, saying prayers and comforting the relatives . . . I must go now—Mother will be frightened if I'm not back soon. She doesn't like being alone any more.
Rowland When will I see you again? Next week here? Or shall I come down with you?
Emmot No, you mustn't do that. Perhaps next week.
Rowland Next week.
Emmot Yes . . . Good-bye, Rowland. Pray for us.
Rowland Emmot . . .

Emmot That's all you can do.

Emmot turns, and walks slowly off

Rowland I must be mad to let her go back.

Slowly Rowland leaves in the opposite direction. Mompesson appears in the church area, wearing his vestments and Emmot reappears with her mother, and they go together to kneel in front of Mompesson, as music begins to play. Simultaneously, Howe, Unwin and Merril enter from different directions, and meet centre, while the rest of the villagers begin to come on and kneel in front of Mompesson, preserving their family groups: Mrs Cooper alone, wearing a black shawl. All the Hancocks, all the Friths, and the Thornleys, Edytha, John, Thomas and Frances Torre, wearing black hoods, John and Deborah Wilson. Elizabeth Swanne, Lydia Chapman, George and Rowland Mower. Catherine Mompesson enters last of all and kneels near to Mompesson, as the music and the section between the three men ends. At the same time, the Bedlam enters, and sits on the pedestal of the cross, playing with a piece of string

Howe Merry Christmas, old men.
Merril Ah.
Unwin What's merry about it?
Howe Mainly that I'm here to see it.
Unwin It may be merry for you.
Merril There'll be no singing in a lot of houses this year!
Unwin There won't!
Howe Ay, but the worst is over now.
Unwin Who told you that?
Howe The plague needs the sun. When the ice comes, he dies.
Unwin The sun will come back.
Howe You're too gloomy, Unwin.
Unwin I've lived a long time.
Howe Well, I reckon he's losing his grip. At the beginning everyone died. Now, some people are recovering.
Unwin Ah, some.
Merril You were lucky, Marshall Howe.
Howe Not only me. I was only ill for two days, and that not very much. He's getting weak, and I was too strong for him. But there was Margaret Blackwell, too.
Unwin That's only two.
Merril What happened to her, then?
Howe She got it two weeks ago, and it was bad. The boils were up and going black, and she was delirious. Her brother gave her up, and went to find the rector. But when he got back, she was much better. Next day she was up, and now she's well.
Merril How did that happen?
Howe They say she had a terrible thirst on her, and her brother not being

there, got out of bed to find a drink. There was a pot of hot bacon fat on the table, straight from the oven, and her being in her mad state, she put it straight down. Must have been that I suppose.

Merril Luck I call that.

Unwin No, no, stands to sense. Fat goes hard when it gets cold, doesn't it? So all the black devils drinking up her blood gets clogged up in it, and they all dies of suffocation, stands to sense. Like I said, it's will-power. If you've got the willpower to go round drinking hot fat all day, scalding your mouth out and all, you're bound to recover. Seems quite logical to me.

Howe Ah, but it proves what I said, too. Next Christmas we'll still be here talking about it.

Unwin I shall be, I know that. It'll take more than plague to get me. But I wouldn't be so sure about you.

Howe Get on with you, Methuselah! You'll be fallen to pieces and gone rotten like an old cowshed before I'm forty!

The three men go and stand at the back of the congregation, just as Mompesson lifts his head to speak

Stanley slips in downstage, just before Mompesson begins

Mompesson Brothers and sisters in God. The day after tomorrow is Christ's birthday. On that day one thousand six hundred and sixty-five years ago he was born in Bethlehem. God stepped from his throne and became a man. He did that for two reasons: to show us, by precept and example, the nature of his Kingdom; and to die. The sun persisted in October, and many of us died, brothers, wives, parents and children. But the lesser sun is down, and the Great Son is rising. He sends us snow and ice to make us clean. The death that has been our companion he is freezing out, and the death of that death is at hand. I ask you, then, on his day, to be sad, and joyful, together: sad that so many have left us; joyful that they are now with him in Paradise. And joyful that what he asked us to endure for his sake, we have endured. And when the continuance of this cold weather puts an end to our sufferings, let us not be afraid to rejoice and give thanks. Let us rejoice on his day, and let the celebration be worthy of the event.

There is a short pause; then Catherine gets up and goes off, and all the villagers rise and begin to leave the stage in different directions. Some gather round Mompesson, and there is even a suggestion of a certain re-strained gaiety. Howe, Unwin and Merril leave together, just in front of the Thornleys, speaking as they go

Howe There you are, Unwin. The rector agrees with me.

Unwin He's a young man.

Howe Hey, what are you doing here, Edward Thornley? Praying with gentlemen and hirelings now are you?

Edward Thornley We prayed in our own hearts in our own way, and we are not defiled.

Howe Oh, I am glad to hear that!

Edward Thornley There is a moment for peace, when all men suffer.

Elizabeth Thornley And we wanted to hear what the rector had to say.

Howe Are you still taking care, Edward, that's what I want to know. Or are you all speaking to each other again?

Edward Thornley My family is safe. I shall keep them that way.

Howe Well, I shall be celebrating, day after tomorrow.

Elizabeth Thornley So will we, Marshall Howe. (*Going*) Edward, there's no need to be so strict now, you heard what the rector said.

Edward Thornley His mouth is not God's oracle.

The Thornleys exit

Howe I'm going home to dinner. Coming Merril?

Merril Ah.

Howe and Merril go

Unwin is left isolated, shouting after them

Unwin You're all mad. The lot of you!

Unwin goes

Mompesson has been talking to some of the villagers. As they leave him, he sees that the Torres are still kneeling. Mompesson crosses to Edytha Torre, and offers her his hand to help her to get up

Mompesson Prayer has done all it can, Mrs Torre.

She gets up and her family gathers round her

Edytha Torre Can there ever be enough, Rector?

Mompesson But life must begin again. There comes a time for relief, even for joy.

Edytha Torre Joy? I'm sixty-five now. Two months ago I lost my only son, my daughter-in-law, my grandson and my husband, all in a few days. We had been married for forty-five years. Must I be joyful and sing at Christmas about that? I'm an old woman, Rector, I can't change that quickly.

Mompesson God in his mercy has spared you, and left three grandchildren for your comfort.

Edytha Torre I would rather have died with my husband. And they are orphans. You're too young to know, Rector. Your own heart hasn't been touched. You've been kind to us, and loved us well, but you can't feel the pain in someone else's flesh. You can only watch it.

Mompesson God's blessing with you, Mrs Torre.

Edytha Torre Thank you, sir.

The Torres go off

Mompesson is now alone, except for Stanley, and the Bedlam who is unseen behind the cross. As Mompesson begins to go, Stanley calls after him

Stanley Mr Mompesson.

Mompesson Good day, Mr Stanley.

Stanley I presumed so far as to stand in the church porch . . .

Mompesson There is no presumption. You are welcome in God's house, and especially at this time.

Stanley Do you think you are wise?

Mompesson What do you mean?

Stanley You tell the people what they want to hear. Not what must be told.

Mompesson I tell them what I think.

Stanley Then you should think again. Do you really think God has finished with us?

Mompesson Do you care, Mr Stanley?

Stanley What do you mean by that, sir?

Mompesson Forty-three Christians are dead, some of whom might have been in church today if your heart had been anything but stone.

Stanley God's hand brings the sword for those who rejected him!

Mompesson Rejected you, Mr Stanley, God is more merciful than you are. I don't need your help now.

Stanley That's plain to see, sir. But they loved me too not many years ago.

Mompesson Be that as it may. I pray for them. I do my best for the dying, and I give comfort. I am a long way yet from their hearts, but I give what I can, and on those terms they have accepted me.

Stanley I'll leave you.

Mompesson No! You think I took the easy way! Do you think I like what I have to do? I am revolted by the continual presence of death and sickness; but you cannot preach the second coming to those whose eyes are blinded by fear!

Stanley If you've taken responsibility, you've no right to deceive them with false hopes.

Mompesson I've every right to do as I think best, Mr Stanley. You are the one without rights, seeing that you chose to surrender them.

Stanley Well, you're up now, Mompesson, and there's no holding you . . .

Mompesson When I asked your help, you turned your back on me. You stood aside and waited for me to crumble, so that you could turn to the people and say, "There's your kingsman, there's your scholar, what is he worth here?" Today I brought them hope, and you bring me the advice I no longer need. Your sin is great, Stanley. There was a beggar lying in the road, but the rabbi turned away his eyes and walked on.

Stanley God will judge me, Mompesson, not you!

Mompesson You have judged yourself by your actions. I have nothing to add.

Stanley Listen . . .

Mompesson I have work to do, sir, good afternoon. (*He begins to go*)

Stanley Listen to me!

Mompesson stops

You are a child in the world, Mompesson, you've spent your life in a cloister, and you know nothing! Perhaps one day you will leave here. Perhaps you will go to London with God secure in your heart, with a message of joy and hope for them. You will stand up, and you will open your love to them, all the secret places of your heart you will offer for them to take and use. And you will become a target, a target for hatred, a target in the stocks for rotten tomatoes and bad eggs, for the louts of every street corner to stand and jeer at. On that day you may return and judge me. Till that day, if you have strength, nourish and keep it, because you have not been tried.

Mompesson Your bitterness is a cancer. Before long it will kill you.

Stanley That is my concern, not yours. Good-bye to you, sir, and God's blessing. We will not meet again.

Mompesson In a small village that is unlikely.

Stanley I vowed long ago never to re-enter that house till it was mine again. I add to that our silence.

Mompesson Really, sir . . .!

Stanley Enough is enough of quarrelling. There need be nothing more between us. Good day.

Mompesson As you wish . . .

George Mower enters in haste

George Mower Rector—Rector!

Mompesson Yes, what is it?

George Mower Tony Blackwell's mother's called for you. Up with him all night she's been.

Mompesson Oh. I see.

Mompesson looks at Stanley, who is expressionless

George Mower Frightened the life out of me she did, with her banging on the door. You don't expect visitors these days.

Mompesson Perhaps you'd like to go, Stanley?

George Mower Oh no, excuse me, Rector, she asked me specially for you.

Stanley You'd better tell her she's mistaken. It's too cold for plague.

Stanley goes off

Mompesson watches him go, then turns to George Mower

Mompesson All right, George, I'll come at once. Come with me to the rectory.

Mompesson and George Mower go off together

The Bedlam emerges from behind the pedestal of the cross where he has been sitting, twisted and still. He hobbles down C

Bedlam Shhhhhh! Listen! Can you hear a banging noise? Bang bang bang bang bang . . . Hammer and nails, working hard . . . Christmas boxes.

The Bedlam laughs foolishly and runs off.

The Lights rise to suggest bright sunlight, and perhaps a little birdsong is heard

Emmot Sydall comes slowly out of a cottage. She is very tired, white-faced, with her dress dirty and crumpled. She looks up at the sun, and goes slowly and sits on the pedestal of the cross

Emmot Thank God for the sun.

Catherine comes on carrying a basket. She sees Emmot and goes over to her

Emmot lifts her head and nods

Catherine Is it finished now?
Emmot Half an hour ago.
Catherine Were you with her all night?
Emmot Yes.
Catherine You shouldn't take the risk.
Emmot You do.
Catherine It's my duty.

Emmot shrugs

Go home to bed now.
Emmot I'm seeing Rowland this afternoon. He came every Sunday, all through the winter. He keeps asking me to go away with him.
Catherine Will you go?

Emmot does not answer

Emmot The worst thing of all, is that—I've lost count.
Catherine What do you mean?
Emmot I can remember when the Wilsons died, because Deborah was the first one I looked after. But I've forgotten some.
Catherine It's sixty-five. Thomas Allen died this morning.
Emmot And Joan.
Catherine Sixty-six.
Emmot I can't remember so many.
Catherine William has been keeping the burial register. It seems the least we can do.
Emmot Perhaps it will go on till there's nothing but bare walls and ruins and ivy.

Catherine God will have mercy.

Emmot Perhaps he has forgotten about us.

Catherine You should go home and sleep now.

Emmot My mother is at home if you want to see her. She never leaves that chair. Except to take flowers to the graveyard.

Catherine I promised I'd bring her a basket of cakes today.

Emmot She won't understand you.

Catherine Nevertheless . . .

Catherine goes off

Emmot remains sitting on the pedestal

Emmot After a time, you become cold. A continuous procession of faces, till each one is the same. The same face. They can't all have been people. To be one day alive, and the next underground in a box. It doesn't make sense . . . (*She gets up and moves downstage*) What shall I say to him? "Yes, I will be your wife, we will go away from here, and it will be as if all this never happened?" But it has happened, there are dead ones to prove it . . . So we can only stand here, like ninepins, and wait for the ball to hit or miss us.

Rowland appears on the rostrum

She looks at him oddly

Rowland I thought I'd missed you.

He begins to go to her, but she stops him

Emmot No. You must keep away from me today.

Rowland Why?

Emmot The plague isn't over.

Rowland But you told me last week . . .

Emmot That was last week. I was up all night with Joan Blackwell.

Rowland What do you mean? You . . . ?

Emmot I've been helping the rector's wife with the sick. Since February.

Rowland (*dumbfounded*) Emmot, have you gone mad?

Emmot Rowland . . .

Rowland Haven't you been in enough danger with your own family . . . ?

Emmot She's a woman of great strength, Rowland, but she needs help. Everyone else is too frightened. I've seen and touched so many poor scabbed bodies, I must be immune by now.

Rowland Then you've done your share. Haven't you suffered enough?

Emmot I'm still alive.

Rowland What did your mother say?

Emmot My mother is a child now. Every day she goes to the churchyard with fresh flowers, and she sits for hours, talking to Father and Ellen and Sarah and John in the ground. She is more with them than us.

Rowland That makes it definite. You must come away!

She seems to ignore him, walking away across the hillside

Emmot It's beautiful today, isn't it? The first warm day of spring.

Rowland Emmot . . .!

Emmot Everything's beginning to grow again now the sun's back. Flowers budding, new leaves, animals coming back to life, toads crawling from under stones; what will happen in June, July, August?

Rowland If we're sensible, we won't wait to find out. Go down now and get your mother, and we'll be away tonight.

Emmot Poor Rowland. I feel sorry for you.

Rowland Emmot, what's wrong with you today?

Emmot Nothing.

Rowland You're so remote.

She turns to face him

Emmot I'm not going to see you any more.

Rowland What?

Emmot There, I've told you. I didn't know how to say it—but suddenly it just came.

Rowland I've listened long enough . . .

Emmot Rowland, don't make it harder.

Rowland For three months you've been putting me off. Every moment you stay down there the danger gets worse. I know what will happen if the plague goes on in the summer!

Emmot Don't, don't . . .

Rowland So go down there now, and get your things. And if you don't come back I'll come down and drag you away!

She bursts out in terrible grief

Emmot Oh Rowland, don't you understand, can't you see what I'm trying to say to you? I want to come with you, I've wanted to ever since the children died. I've seen terrible things in the village, things that make me an old woman only to think of them. I'm frightened, I have nightmares full of scabs and oozing wounds every night of my life. I don't want to die yet, I want to come with you!

Rowland Then come.

Emmot I can't, don't you understand, I can't!

Rowland (*doggedly*) I'm sorry, Emmot, I don't see why you can't come.

Emmot Are you too stupid to guess why, must I tell you in words of one syllable?

Rowland looks hurt and hangs his head. Immediately she goes to him and embraces him

I'm sorry, Rowland, I shouldn't have said that.

Rowland Emmot . . .

Emmot And I shouldn't have let you touch me. It's going to be even harder to go now.

Rowland Then don't go.

Emmot I must, I've said so.

Rowland You still haven't told me why.

Emmot Oh Rowland . . .!! After Father and the children died, I asked Mother to come away. One night, I even pretended we were going for a walk together, but when we got to the edge of the village, she turned round and ran back. I almost came by myself that night. I kept on asking, day in and day out. But she doesn't understand . . . She says she won't leave Father and the children.

Rowland But they're dead!

Emmot No. Not to her. It's no good, Rowland.

Rowland Doesn't she understand? We're still alive!

Emmot I can't leave her like that, can I? I thought of coming by myself, but it's hopeless. If I left her, she'd starve.

Rowland Can't we do anything?

Emmot If we took her away by force, she'd come back. When I realized I'd have to stay, I started helping. The only alternative was to sit and hate her more and more.

Rowland Leave her, Emmot. You've done all you can.

Emmot No. I can do more yet. And I'm dangerous now. That's why you mustn't see me any more.

Rowland But other people come in: the Hancocks from Riley.

Emmot We've not seen them since Christmas.

Rowland We can't be parted indefinitely, Emmot. Does it matter that much?

Emmot You haven't seen it! It does matter, Rowland. What could I say if you took it from me back to Middleton?

Pause

Rowland I'm frightened to leave you down there, Emmot.

Emmot God has spared me so far.

Rowland Don't go near the sick ones, please.

Emmot They don't frighten me now. They're only poor people who are ill. They need help.

Rowland When will I see you again?

Emmot I don't know. When it's over.

Rowland Emmot . . .

Emmot Go now, Rowland, each minute makes it worse.

Rowland Let me kiss you at least . . .

Silently she holds out her hand. He takes it and kisses it. It is a moment of stilted formality, full of emotion

Emmot Go home now. Don't turn back.

She turns away from him. He looks at her for a moment, then turns and walks back towards the exit. He turns back and looks at her

Rowland Good-bye, Emmot.

She stays turned away from him.

Emmot Good-bye.

Rowland goes off

Dear God, why must I send him away? Why must we be tied, like slaves? Those iron reasons for staying, so logical and binding. Tomorrow morning they'll seem fragile and empty as eggshells.

Slowly Emmot leaves the stage

The Lights illuminate the whole stage

Colonel and Mrs Bradshaw enter together, carrying between them a large amount of luggage

Mrs Bradshaw Let's stop for a minute, I must have a rest. (*She sits on a case*) Oh dear, it's so hot.
Colonel Bradshaw Not a soul in sight, either—oh, wait a minute. Hey, you!

Edward Thornley enters, followed by the other five Thornleys

Edward Thornley Good morning, Colonel.
Colonel Carry these bags down to the crossroads for us. It'll be worth a shilling to you.
Edward Thornley I don't need a shilling today.
Colonel Oh well, there are plenty who do . . .

As Colonel Bradshaw looks round the five Hancocks, led by William, enter at another corner

Hey you, Hancock! Carry these bags to the crossroads for me.
William Hancock Not today, Colonel.

Colonel Bradshaw looks round again

The seven Friths, led by George, enter at another corner, and the remaining villagers appear from different areas, to complete a half-circle enclosing the Bradshaws. The remaining villagers are: Edytha, John, Thomas and Frances Torre; Howe; Unwin and Merril; Mrs Cooper; Elizabeth Swanne; Lydia Chapman; Rowland and George Mower, and the Bedlam, who takes no part in the following, but sits on the pedestal watching and reacting

Colonel What's going on here? What are you all doing out in the street?
Edward Thornley We heard you were going away.
William Hancock We've come to see you off.
George Frith And to give you our best wishes.
Colonel What's it got to do with you?

Edward Thornley Nothing at all, Colonel.

William Hancock We're just interested.

Colonel It's none of your business. Well, won't any of you carry these bags? Can't you see my wife is tired? What are you all staring at?

Mrs Bradshaw Never mind, I'll carry them. Let's get away from here.

Colonel and Mrs Bradshaw pick up their bags with difficulty, watched by the silent crowd, and move towards the exit. As they do so, the circle of people tightens round them. Mrs Bradshaw looks round, frightened. They stop, as Edward Thornley bars their way

Colonel You're in my way.

Edward Thornley That's right.

Colonel Get out, let me pass.

Edward Thornley We want to know where you're going.

Colonel That's none of your business.

William Hancock We think it is.

Colonel Let me pass I say!

George Frith We're waiting.

Colonel I'm going away on business—to Sheffield on business . . .

Edward Thornley With all those cases?

George Frith And your wife?

William Hancock Leaving your house open and empty?

Edward Thornley Liar!

Colonel How dare you . . .!

William Hancock Where are you going?

An angry murmur from the crowd

Mrs Bradshaw For Heaven's sake, tell them.

Colonel I don't see why I should be bullied like this . . .

Mrs Bradshaw We're going to London till the plague's over.

Silence

Colonel Yes. Since you insist. We're staying there with some friends till the danger is over here. Now, if you'd kindly let us pass . . .

Edward Thornley What about us?

Colonel I don't see what you mean . . .

William Hancock What about the rest of us?

Colonel Well, really, that's hardly my concern, is it . . .?

George Frith You're running away!

Edward Thornley Leaving us to die and be damned.

William Hancock What about our lives?

George Frith Our wives and children?

Edward Thornley What do you care about us?

An angry roar from the crowd. Colonel Bradshaw tries hard to preserve his dignity, but the crowd, now dominated by the men, is getting closer

Stanley enters and watches

Colonel What you do is up to you. If you're sensible, you'll leave while you can.

Edward Thornley We've got nowhere to go!

George Frith We're poor people.

William Hancock We haven't got town houses and rich friends in London.

Colonel You must fend for yourselves as best you can, like I'm doing . . .

Edward Thornley You're staying here, Colonel!

William Hancock You can stick it out, like we have to.

Colonel You can't do this, you've no right . . .!

Stanley turns away as if to go off

Edward Thornley You're prepared to leave us here to rot without a second thought, aren't you. Are we going tò let him get away with that?

All No, no!

Colonel As the first citizen of this village——

Edward Thornley (*cutting in*) Yes, the first to run away!

Colonel —I command you to let me pass!

Edward Thornley Stop him!

Colonel Bradshaw attempts to break through. Immediately the circle closes on the two of them. Fear has made the crowd ready for any scapegoat, and it is a very ugly moment. As the circle closes, Mrs Bradshaw catches sight of Stanley going away

Mrs Bradshaw Mr Stanley . . .!

The crowd closes in, and Colonel Bradshaw and his wife are borne under a mass of arms and fists. Mrs Bradshaw screams from within the circle. Stanley has heard her cry for help. His immediate reaction is to hurry away, but he stops, undecided. Then he hears her scream, and suddenly, almost in spite of himself, he calls out

Stanley Stop! In the name of God, stop it!

There is a sudden hush, and all heads turn towards Stanley. For a moment there is silence, as he faces the large crowd alone. Through the legs of the crowd the two Bradshaws are visible on the floor amid their bags

Have you all gone mad?

Edward Thornley We have just cause, Mr Stanley.

Stanley There is no just cause for this! Stand back.

Stanley moves across and the crowd falls back. The Bradshaws pick themselves up

Are you all right?

Colonel I have survived worse things than the mob, Stanley.

An angry murmur from the crowd. They prepare to move in again

Stanley God's eye is upon you, he will not forgive this!

The crowd subsides

Edward Thornley They're running away, Mr Stanley.

William Hancock They don't care about us.

George Frith We can stay here and die.

William Hancock They'll be safe in London.

Edward Thornley We were only trying to stop them.

Stanley With your fists and boots? You won't kill the plague by fighting them, nor conquer your own fear with violence. That needs a faith which you have lost.

Edward Thornley But, sir . . .

Stanley They have a perfect right to go if they please. You know that, all of you.

Francis Frith Is it right that they should go when we have to stay?

Colonel No-one has to stay.

William Hancock We can't afford to do otherwise.

Colonel Look, this is my home, too, as well as yours! But I'd rather leave here and stay alive, than stay here and die!

Edward Thornley All right, then why don't we all go? If he can run fast, I can run faster!

Stanley No, listen to me . . .

William Hancock We've had our example, Stanley, we've seen the light . . .

A roar of approval from the crowd

Stanley Your example is a bad one, the coward's way . . .

Colonel The way to live, sir.

Stanley But the plague is with you now, already . . .

Colonel All the more reason for going.

Stanley If you leave here you will take the death with you, in your belongings, on your clothes, in the very words you speak. If you want to give an example, Colonel——

Colonel (*cutting in*) It's not Sunday, sir, I'm in no mood for sermons.

Stanley Then go, sir, with your tail between your legs. I have told you what's right.

Colonel You told us what was right for twenty years, and our lives were misery. This time I'll decide for myself.

The Bradshaws pick up their bags

I'll be back next year to put flowers on your graves.

The Bradshaws begin to go. The crowd murmurs angrily

Stanley Let them go.

The Bradshaws go off

The crowd boos

Edward Thornley If they can go, so can we.

Stanley No, listen, listen to me . . .

William Hancock We've had our example, Mr Stanley.

The crowd begins to disperse rapidly in all directions

Stanley You can't run away from dying, you can only move to another place, another place to end in, another place to dig the same grave . . .!

But no-one listens. They all go off except Howe, Unwin and Merril, and the Bedlam sitting on the pedestal

Howe Save your breath, Stanley. When the river's on the ebb you must swim with it.
Stanley Will you go too, then?
Howe No, I have some judgement left. When all our infected neighbours are gone, this will be the safest place.
Unwin They're all mad. You won't go, will you, Merril?
Merril I'd rather die in bed than on the roadside.
Unwin Ah. Me too.
Stanley At every village and inn where they pause for breath, they will leave their mark.
Howe A ring of roses on the landlord's cheek.
Unwin They're fools to run. No-one will take them in when they know they're from Eyam.
Stanley If only they could be made to stay, here in the village . . .
Howe Oh aye, that's likely. It takes a brave man to sign his own death sentence. If you could call out all Cromwell's dead soldiers, Stanley, you might have a chance then!
Stanley Somehow . . .
Howe It'll be a nice quiet village with just the four of us.
Unwin Are you coming, Marshall Howe, or will you talk all day?
Howe Aye, I'm coming.

Howe, Unwin and Merril exit, followed by the Bedlam

Stanley is left alone. The Lights concentrate on him, as he is swept by an inner excitement. He looks round at the empty streets and shuttered houses, arguing the matter out with himself in a tense sotto voce

Stanley Or persuaded . . . Yes, persuaded, to make the choice from their own hearts! . . . But no. No. It never happens. Don't men always choose the easy way, haven't I reason enough to know it, who watched our soldiers' revolution collapse into tyranny . . .? Yes, in those days it could have happened. Anything was possible then! In those days I spoke like a prophet, and how they listened, those pikemen with the blood fresh on their jerkins, those troops of Levellers, with pamphlets in their helmets and their fists pledged for revolution! I held them spellbound, with a picture of the world as it is going to be! . . . So why not now? . . . (*Dawning*) With Mompesson . . . Together . . . Yes—together . . . Together.

Much happens to Stanley in the space of those three "togethers". There is

a look on his face we have not seen before and he turns briskly and walks into the rectory area

> *The Lights come on, and Mompesson appears, so that we are into the scene with the least possible delay*

Mompesson Stanley!
Stanley The room hasn't changed. Only the tenant.
Mompesson It is fruitless, sir, to pursue that argument.
Stanley I made a vow once. But I made it in bitterness. I hope you will forgive me.

Mompesson is completely taken aback

Mompesson Willingly, sir . . .
Stanley There are differences between us, let us not forget that.
Mompesson Your feelings are mine, Stanley, you need not put them into words . . .
Stanley As long as it is understood, sir . . .
Mompesson It is understood.
Stanley Then perhaps we can at least speak together. Have you been into the village this morning?
Mompesson No, not yet. There is a problem I must solve that has kept me at my table most of the night.
Stanley The Bradshaws left. The whole village is ready to follow them.
Mompesson Yes, that was it.
Stanley If they run away the infection will spread!
Mompesson There is only one answer, Stanley. The enormity of it staggers me.
Stanley What?
Mompesson The village must be enclosed, with guards posted, and I must enforce a discipline as strict as if this were war. No-one must enter or leave till the plague is over. It's easy to plan, but it cannot be enforced. We would need the best part of a regiment.
Stanley No, no, it can be done without soldiers.
Mompesson How?
Stanley Enforcement is no answer. It must be done voluntarily.
Mompesson Voluntarily? There is no chance of that, surely.
Stanley There is a chance. If anyone on earth can do it, perhaps we can.
Mompesson I did think of speaking to the people. But you know the difficulties I have here. There are still many people to whom my word is nothing. They would ignore me.
Stanley Your word need not be alone, Mompesson. There is my word to stand with it.

A short pause, as they both begin to see each other in a new light

Stanley Is it possible?
Mompesson I don't know. It could be tried.

Stanley Together we have the whole spiritual guidance of the village. We could never exploit it to better purpose.

Mompesson If we are right. Because if we do this, we will condemn many people to death.

Stanley If we don't do it, it could be thousands. At the worst it would be hundreds here.

Mompesson It's easy to speak of figures, but when they are dead in our hands . . .

Stanley We will endure it, as they do.

Mompesson Yes, if a man were made of iron . . .

Stanley He can be stronger than that.

Mompesson Well. We shall see. Our strength or weakness won't be in question if we can't persuade the people.

Stanley When I was young I could have done it. Then there was fire on my lips. Now, my mouth has been closed so long, I don't know what will come out. Eloquence, or ashes.

Mompesson God must give us strength.

Stanley We have that. We need the words.

Stanley and Mompesson exit quickly, as though into the rectory

Immediately, the Bedlam jumps up from behind the cross, and begins running across the stage shouting in all directions

Bedlam Everybody! Everybody! Crawl out of your houses, like rats from under the straw! Come and stand on your graves!

Edward Thornley and the five members of his family enter. They are all carrying rolled-up bundles of luggage

Bedlam Mister, hey, mister!

Edward Thornley Out of my way, boy, I'm in a hurry.

Bedlam The rector wants you to come to the churchyard to talk about the plague.

Edward Thornley Well he can go on wanting.

Elizabeth Thornley Edward, we ought to go, just to see . . .

William Thornley It might be important.

Edward Thornley All right then. But only for a few minutes.

Mompesson and Stanley have come on together outside the rectory area, and have their heads bowed in prayer. The Thornleys cross to stand in front of them, putting down their bags. The other villagers are already entering and joining them. First Howe, Unwin and Merril, Mrs Cooper, Elizabeth Swanne, Lydia Chapman, Rowland and George Mower

The Bedlam stands up C, dancing around and waving his hands, in the midst of the tide of people converging on the rectory area

Bedlam Here they come, here they come, all the people! There's going to be a party!

The Bedlam runs off up C. *The families are entering. The five remaining Torres, the Hancocks and the Friths. They all gather round the rostrum on which the two clergymen are standing, the whole village, and Mompesson and Stanley still in prayer*

Elizabeth Thornley Look, Edward, there's Mr Stanley, right next to the rector.

Edward Thornley That's a surprise.

The villagers are all in position. The two men look up. There is silence

Mompesson I asked you to come here because there is something that must be said.

Edward Thornley If you're going to tell us we've got the plague, Rector, we already know.

Murmurs from the crowd, growing louder

Mompesson You must listen to me . . .

Edward Thornley Then hurry up, Rector, because we're not staying long here.

Loud approval

Mompesson The bags at your feet have already told me that, and I can see clearly enough that everyone here agrees with you. But you are wrong! It is my duty to tell you directly and to your faces that you are wrong . . .

Edward Thornley You're too late, we've already decided. Come on, let's go . . .

Stanley Wait! Your life is packed in those bags, and if you value it, you must listen to what we have to say.

Pause. Loud murmuring and chattering

Mompesson There is only one thing that needs to be said here. You have not thought what it will mean if you run away.

William Hancock It will mean saving our lives, we've thought that much.

Mompesson No! Your lives are already on the scale, they've been there since the day you were born, leaving here will not change that!

Francis Frith The plague is here, nowhere else. I'm not going to stay here and be killed when I could be safe outside!

Stanley There is no safety outside. Wherever you are, there the plague is. For ten months it's been in this village. Do you think, because you are not dead, that you've been left unmarked? It's in every fold of your skin, you leave its fingermark on everything you touch.

Mompesson The plague is nowhere else but here, you admit it, Francis Frith. But if you go, the plague goes with you. Every house you enter, every person you speak to, will be infected when you leave!

Edward Thornley Our lives are at stake. If we stay here we'll die!

Mompesson That's in God's hands, no action of yours can change it. If you go, you'll die in the next valley instead of this one, and there others will die with you.

Stanley How many murderers have we here? How many men who will stick a knife into a friend's back, or beat a child's head to fragments with a spade, or poison a woman for money? There's no difference. If others die outside this village, the blood will be on your hands!

Mompesson If you leave here, you will scatter the seeds of this pestilence on every wind that blows: and tomorrow the black spot may be growing on a thousand faces . . .

Stanley There is no running, only to run from God, no flying, only to fly from death, which is the prescribed ending, written for all men. God has driven us to the wall, and asked us to stand for His sake. Who here will say no?

A confused and disturbed chattering. George Frith calls above it

George Frith What can we do, Rector? Are you asking us to stay here and die?

A loud reaction, with a great deal of angry dissent. It is now or never, as Stanley faces their anger, the orator's passion lifting him to meet the situation once again

Stanley Is there any choice? We are born to it, from the cradle. As a father apprentices his son to his own trade, we are all apprenticed to this trade of living. To pass from childhood into strength, to live for a few years in the flowering and richness of being man, and then to drop and wrinkle into age and dotage. To watch, with a brain that is still sharp, the slow droop and wither of what was once firm into mould and decay, to watch it, unable to prevent, and to acquiesce at last in the death all our ingenuity and care cannot postpone by one day, one hour. At a certain time, a day of high wind, or rain, when the sun is up, or sinking, a time irrelevant and reasonless, the machine stops, and there is no mechanic born who can set again those wheels in motion. Like our fathers and grandfathers, like the fathers before them, back into the first depths and unremembered beginnings of time, we end, and that ending is omega on this earth, the last full stop on the last page of our years. You can run till your heart bursts, but your shadow will stay with you while the sun shines, and when it sinks, the darkness is absolute.

A shattered silence. Edward Thornley speaks quietly

Edward Thornley We know we can't shake him off, Mr Stanley. But must we turn and embrace him, too?

Stanley Leave if you will, but you will find all gates barred to you, guards on the road to turn you back. No town will accept a leper, nor welcome the infected. You will be forced to live in caves, like animals, and when you die, you will die in ditches, with no help, and no prayers. If you leave here, you condemn yourselves to exile, the outcast life of a beggar. Go to Sheffield. Bang on the city walls! You will find pikemen, and muskets levelled at your chest.

A burst of chatter and murmuring

William Hancock What should we do, Rector? You called this meeting. Was it only to tell us to go home and die?

Mompesson Stanley is right. This is our place, or our prison. We have no choice but to stay.

Edward Thornley The Bradshaws had a choice! No-one stopped them!

A roar of approval from the crowd

Stanley Yes, and you have a choice too Edward Thornley, every man has a choice!

A moment of uncertainty in the crowd. Stanley rams home his advantage

Yes, Edward, I'm speaking to you. Since when has Colonel Bradshaw been your example?

Edward Thornley Mr Stanley . . . !

Stanley Did you stand at Bradshaw's side at Marston Moor?

Edward Thornley I did not! I stood for the Parliament, then and now!

Stanley And do you remember how it was?

Edward Thornley I'll never forget that day.

Stanley When both wings were in disorder, and only the centre stood between the King and victory. A long hour we stood there, Edward, bracing our pikes till our arms were breaking, while the King's troopers came at us, again, and again, and again! But for an hour we held on. We didn't turn and run, like some others did, and that endurance won us the day. Isn't that how it was, Edward?

Edward Thornley Aye, that's how it was . . .

Stanley Yes, Edward. You have a choice. Every man has a choice. You made it that day, and you'll make it again, now!

Pause. Thornley is transfixed. Mompesson seizes the chance

Mompesson We have made a plan, which will make what we have to suffer easier to bear . . .

Murmurs, "What is it, tell us", etc., from the crowd

From today, till the plague is over, the village must be enclosed.

Murmurs, "No, no, what do you mean, be quiet, listen"

We will draw a boundary line of stones around us, and until we are sure that the plague has finished its work here, that line must never be crossed. Neither will we go out, nor will any stranger come in.

Restrained reaction, as it sinks in

Mompesson I shall write a letter today to the Lord Lieutenant asking him for a supply of food to be left for us each day. On the day his letter returns, our gates will be closed.

Francis Frith And that'll be the end of us!

Loud reaction

Stanley Your sacrifice is ours, too! If you will stay, we will take on our shoulders the generalship of this battle. As in all battles, some will die, and leaders are not bullet proof!

Mompesson I can see the fear in your faces. There is fear in my heart, too, we are liars if we don't confess it.

Stanley But with your help, we can win. We can give our enemy the bare minimum of sacrifice he demands.

Mompesson The time is now, and the answer is in your hands.

A low murmur of concerned and wavering talk. Then Edward Thornley speaks in a loud voice, crossing to Stanley

Edward Thornley You can unpack those bags. I stood at your side at Marston Moor, Mr Stanley, and I'll not desert you now. We'll stay.

Loud reaction. Francis Frith and some others shout "No"

George Frith And us.

William Hancock We'll stay, too.

Mompesson Will anyone go? Turn now, in the eyes of all of us.

Pause. No-one moves

Edward Thornley We'll all stay, Rector. If that's what you think best.

Mompesson We will have a meeting in the rectory in an hour's time. If the head of every family in the village will come, we can discuss the details of our plan.

Silence

Thank you for listening to us for so long. Go home now, and ask God for the strength we will all need.

Edward Thornley Amen!

Others in the Crowd Amen, amen . . .

The crowd goes slowly, drifting away almost in silence. There is nothing to say. They bend and pick up their bags, husbands put their hands on wives' shoulders, and they slowly disperse to all corners of the stage. The Bedlam wanders among them as they go, chuckling to himself and pointing to them, muttering gibberish

Catherine remains alone, away from the two men. All the villagers are gone. There is a moment of absolute silence. The two men look at each other, realizing perhaps for the first time the full implication of their action

Stanley God help us, Mompesson. What have we done?

CURTAIN

ACT III

The CURTAIN *rises on a tableau. Merril sits on the pedestal, looking up into the sky, listening. There is a noise of digging. Most of the villagers are facing offstage watching the burial: the seven Friths; the five Hancocks; Edytha, John, Thomas and Frances Torre; Elizabeth Swanne; Lydia Chapman; Rowland and George Mower, and Mrs Cooper. Unwin sits alone on a bench, drinking from a bottle. A few seconds after the* CURTAIN *rises, Marshall Howe and the Bedlam enter together, or are discovered*

Howe It's a hot day for digging, isn't it, boy?

Bedlam I've been watching an ant building a house.

Howe They're building houses in Thornley's field. Two narrow houses, six foot deep. One room and a bed for the night.

Bedlam They was all in a line, walking along, with grass and straw. They went in a hole by the corner of the wall.

Howe How many more of us will end up sleeping in that field?

Bedlam I kicked it all up, to see what was inside. And they ran about all over the place.

Howe Or will we be dead in the streets, and unburied?

Bedlam So I trod on them. They was all on their backs, waving their broken little legs, and all crying.

Howe Ants don't make noises.

Bedlam It was very quiet.

The spade noise ceases. Merril gets up and comes down to Howe

Howe Have they finished yet?

Merril Saying the prayers. Sad it should come to this.

Unwin gets up from the bench and joins them, still holding the bottle, and slightly tipsy

Unwin It's not sad at all, it's common sense. The graveyard's full.

Howe Eighty-two graves in nine months.

Merril I always thought I'd be buried decently, not in a field.

Unwin No point in thinking any more, Andrew Merril. Drinking, more like. You always were a bit slow cottoning on.

Unwin exits unsteadily

Howe What's wrong with the old man today? He doesn't usually drink so much?

Merril It's old Isaac Thornley being buried. We were always together, you know, us three, when we were lads. Shakes you up when your friends die, even if you're as old as I am. Shakes you up . . .

Howe Ah. I know.

Merril Time to take steps, that's what it is.

Howe Eh?

Merril Like Emmot Sydall's mother. Gone up to the hills she has, all by herself. They say she lives like a madwoman in a cave, just inside the stones.

Howe You won't last long in a cave.

Merril I've got more sense than that. But you've seen the last of me here till it's over. I'm going to build a hut.

Howe At your age?

Merril I'm old, but I'm not weak. I've taken the wood already, up on to the moor. I'm taking some hens and the old cockerel, and the goat . . .

Howe If Noah could build an ark at five hundred, I expect you'll manage.

Merril You'll do the same, if you're wise.

Howe I've got a wife and boy to contend with.

Merril Ah. Please yourself, then. I'll see you when it's over. If you're lucky.

Merril exits

Howe Ah. Mebbe.

George Mower Here they come . . .

Edward, William, Francis and Mary Thornley enter, wearing their hats and black cloaks

The villagers draw back a little, but there is no panic

George Frith God be with you, Edward.

Pause, as Thornley looks at them

Edward Thornley Haven't you got anything better to do than stand in the street gaping?

Elizabeth Swanne We are offering our prayers.

Edward Thornley They come too late for us. Go home.

Francis Frith That's what you did, Edward, but it didn't help!

Edward Thornley Leave us alone.

Francis Frith No, I won't!

George Frith Be quiet, Francis!

Francis Frith I won't be quiet, we've all gone mad! Five people who were at that meeting are already dead!

George Frith We know the risk.

Francis Frith You stay then. I'm going!

Edward Thornley You're staying with the rest of us.

Francis Frith You speak for yourself!

Edward Thornley I'm speaking for you, too!

Francis Frith You're the maddest of the lot, Edward Thornley. Three of your family are dead since that meeting, and you're still blind!

Edward Thornley I'm still of the same mind, if that's what you mean. (*He looks round at them all*) And I say that no-one leaves now, not while I'm here to stop him!

Francis Frith Which won't be long!

George Frith And so do I!

Francis Frith Listen, Father——

George Frith (*cutting in*) Be quiet, son!

Francis Frith We're all mad, mad . . .

Mompesson and Catherine enter at the end of this exchange, as though from the burial

Francis Thornley has been standing with his family, unobtrusively rubbing his forehead. Suddenly he sneezes loudly. Then again, and a third time. There is dead silence, as everyone looks at him. He whispers

Francis Thornley God help me—God help me . . . (*He sneezes again*)

Sudden uproar in the crowd. They disperse in all directions, leaving only Mompesson and Catherine, and the Thornleys. Edward puts his arm round his son's shoulder. Francis Frith shouts as he leaves

Francis Frith (*going*) I told you, I told you! There's the next one!

As the Thornleys leave, Catherine moves away from Mompesson, and stands with her back to him

Mompesson God's mercy with you.

Edward Thornley Ay, sir, that's the point.

The Thornleys exit, helping Francis

Mompesson and Catherine are left alone. Mompesson turns and sees her standing apart

Mompesson Catherine?

She turns and looks at him in silence

Catherine? What is it?

Catherine Nothing.

She turns away from him and walks quickly into their house area. He follows her at once

Mompesson Catherine, what's wrong?

Catherine It's nothing, leave me alone.

Mompesson Tell me.

Catherine It's no good, William.

Mompesson What do you mean?

Catherine All this. It's no good.

Mompesson I don't understand you.

Catherine Didn't you see it, then?

Mompesson Catherine . . .

Catherine That scrawny old man we wrapped in a blanket yesterday. And the son, looking at his dead wife, pretending to be strong! And now the next one, publicly, in the street, beginning to die. He'll be buried the day after tomorrow, and by that time, somewhere in the village, there'll be two or three others touching their scabs.

Mompesson We've got to be strong.

Catherine Strong! All this doesn't matter if we're strong. All the agony and the suffering and the death is cancelled out if we're strong. We show nothing on our faces, we just nod and count up on our fingers as the next one dies. We might as well be stones.

Mompesson Catherine, you know as well as I do . . .

Catherine I don't want to be strong any more. I want to be weak. I want to be human again!

Mompesson What are you saying?

Catherine I'm saying must I go in to our children and say to them, my darlings, you're only four and five, but your father says you must be strong, so that if you die next week, without having had any life, you mustn't mind, because that's what God wants. I don't care any more what God wants, I want my children to live, I want to get away from this awful place where living is all sickness and bodies, and shallow graves dug in a field. I've tried with all my heart, but I can't endure it any more, I can't . . .

She sits at the table and cries uncontrollably. He stands above her with his hand on her shoulder

Mompesson It's easy to speak, even easy to convince people, if you chose your words. After that comes the action. It frightens me to think what we've done.

The Lights cross-fade, leaving Mompesson and Catherine half-lit, and revealing Stanley alone on the other side of the stage

Stanley Between the decision and the action, there's always time for thought. When the sum of the dead is completed, what shall I say? That these ended, became names in an old book, because my pride loved the sound of its own voice? Better never begin, let chance scatter death as it will, than that.

The Lights cross-fade, revealing Mompesson and Catherine again. She has stopped crying

Catherine I keep seeing my two children put dead into a box. What will I say to you then? Because that life is my life, and if you kill it——

Mompesson (*cutting in*) I kill it! Catherine!

Catherine We must pack our bags and go, in secret, at night if necessary, go somewhere where we can live and love God, not be forced to hate him.

Mompesson Go? After everything that's happened? It was you in the beginning who told me . . .

Catherine That was in the beginning. It was easy to say do this or that before we knew what the words meant. Does everything we have belong to other people, is nothing at all our own?

Pause

Mompesson What can I say? There is instinct on the one hand, and logic on the other. When they collide, it's always logic that is destroyed.

Catherine What shall we do?

Mompesson In my study, when I read of heroes, I always wondered what it must be like: tremendous freedom and joy, surely? The truth is much more prosaic. Nothing more than being forced by circumstances to do something you'd much rather avoid.

The Lights cross-fade to Stanley, as before

Stanley For me, the choice is easy. I've nowhere to go, not much lifetime left to save, and I'd rather stay here and take my chance. But the others, the young, who stand to lose everything. What a weight of guilt for one man's back when he's called to stand before God. "Dear Father, I killed all those people, because I thought it was for the best." It will sound like nonsense . . . A great stone is beginning to roll. Perhaps there is still time to stop it before it crushes us all.

Suddenly decisive, Stanley goes briskly off

The Lights cross-fade back to Mompesson and Catherine

Catherine What shall we do, William? Everything's confused.

Mompesson I've been selfish. You must go with the children.

Catherine I didn't mean that . . .

Mompesson I've no right to ask you to stay . . .

Catherine William, I meant both of us, not just me, together.

Mompesson But that would make everything I've ever said lies and hypocrisy!

Pause

Catherine Would it be hypocrisy to send the children away?

Mompesson Without you?

Catherine Yes, without me.

Mompesson I don't know. I said there could be no exceptions.

Catherine Most of the children were sent away months ago. And the ones who stayed are dead now.

Mompesson But what would the villagers say?

Catherine I suppose they would object—if they knew . . .

Mompesson You're not suggesting . . .?

Catherine My children are my children.

Mompesson But that would be wrong, deception . . .

Catherine Can a child of four decide? Or is decision forced upon him? You said it must be done voluntarily.

Mompesson Yes, I know . . .

Catherine Or not at all.

Mompesson Yes.

Catherine Our children are too young to judge. If we keep them here, is morality squared? When they are buried, will your conscience be satisfied?

Mompesson Catherine, this is sophistry, they may be infected.

Catherine I can't stay here and watch them die!

Mompesson Do you think I can?

Pause

Catherine If they were safely away, we would be certain then. When we've done so much for other people, one small thing for ourselves . . .

Mompesson One small betrayal.

Catherine If it were to make our purpose stronger?

Mompesson Could it be justified, even then?

But Catherine can see that his resolution is already nine-tenths broken

Catherine (*quietly*) It must be justified, William. It must be.

Mompesson (*after a short pause, quietly*) Pack a bag for them. I'll see them carried to your brother in Yorkshire tonight.

Catherine Yes . . .

Mompesson After midnight, when all honest men are asleep.

Catherine Yes . . . (*Slowly*) I wonder if I will ever see them again?

A knock at the door. Mompesson starts guiltily

Mompesson Who's that? (*He opens the door*)

Stanley enters

Stanley.

Stanley Good evening. Can I speak to you for a few moments?

Mompesson Of course. Come in.

Catherine goes out as Stanley comes in

Between the two men there seems to be a faint echo of their former hostility

Mompesson How are you, Stanley?

Stanley Well enough, thank you.

Mompesson What did you want?

Stanley I thought we ought to confer again. To see if things still stand where we left them.

Mompesson The Duke's letter came this afternoon.

Stanley What does he say?

Mompesson He will help us in every way he can. He writes many fine words about our courage. Fine words are easy to write.

Stanley Is that your feeling, too?

Mompesson I—don't know what you mean.

Stanley Action should be taken in the heat. Since we spoke to the people, I have often thought . . .

Mompesson What?

Stanley What you implied when you spoke of fine words.

Mompesson I implied nothing.

Stanley Nevertheless, I'll tell you what's in my mind. At the meeting, we convinced people, and as we spoke, I suppose we were convinced, too. In the heat of the moment, what we said seemed full of strength. But since then, I have been forced to think . . .

Mompesson About what?

Stanley The wisdom of our choice.

Mompesson As you yourself said, there is no choice.

Stanley Yes, but since then . . .

Mompesson You wish to retract?

Stanley I didn't say that.

Mompesson If you talk of implications . . .

Stanley Have you had no doubts since that day?

Pause. Mompesson's mind is full of his plan to send his children away

Mompesson No. No doubts.

Stanley This last week has been torture to me. Supposing we are wrong? Any man can be wrong. Supposing the plague is only strong because we confine it? Perhaps if we scattered it, the infection would die out . . .

Mompesson Perhaps is speculation, and therefore pointless. We made our choice.

Stanley If we are wrong, we have a lot to answer for. Perhaps the whole village dead.

Mompesson We are not wrong.

Stanley I came to you looking for assurance . . .

Mompesson You have it. We are not wrong.

Stanley We go ahead then?

Mompesson This evening. If you agree.

Stanley I agree. I can do nothing else.

Mompesson I think we should close the church. We could continue to meet in the open, the place the villagers call the Delph. There's more room there for them to sit apart from each other . . . As for burials— we must do what we can. (*Pause*) I'm sorry if I seem brusque with you— but my mind is full tonight.

Stanley We made no compact to be friends.

Mompesson No. Allies.

Stanley nods

If you will take the western part of the village, across Fiddlers Bridge, I will see to the eastern part. It will be safer than calling a meeting.

Stanley What shall I tell them?

Mompesson Tell them what we decided about the church, and to stay locked in their houses from now on, unless called out by us; and tell them that from tomorrow morning the village will be closed.

Stanley Very well. (*He begins to go*)

Mompesson And Stanley.

Stanley Yes?

Mompesson Tell them we will win.

Stanley Yes.

Stanley goes. Catherine enters and stands in the doorway leading to the inner room

Catherine The bags are packed. They're ready.

Mompesson looks at her for a second, and they exit together

The Lights come up, revealing the whole stage, representing the village main street. The stage action during the next scene shows the village during the first weeks of its enclosure. People come out of their houses only when they have to, and move quickly and hooded about their business. Some tentatively look out, and scurry to the well and back for water; others carry or wheel their dead towards the fields. Single figures walk sadly and alone along the street, deep in their private despair. We see, if possible inside and outside the houses, the slow ordeal of waiting and the death. Music may perhaps be used, to accentuate the stylization of the scene

Marshall Howe enters alone

Howe So now the gates are closed. And the ordeal begins. Grass grows in the empty streets, you can almost see it growing, as the sun pours down on our sweating, infested cottages. Shut in our own families, rarely going out, seeing no-one, man, woman and child, each one faces his own terror. We shutter our hearts, and lock away hope, and die as best we can, as the hot days intensify the slaughter. The last coffins were made in June, when the bodies multiplied faster than one man's hands could work, and in July those hands too were stilled. From that time on, it was sheets, old clothes, sacking, anything to cover the scarred nakedness of the beloved dead.

The Bedlam enters quickly, and scurries across to Marshall Howe

Hallo, boy. What's the news among the madmen?

Bedlam The fields are winning.

Howe How's that?

Bedlam There's a lawn growing on the high street.

Howe No carts rolling. No feet to walk, only the slow processions of the dead.

Bedlam No-one speaks to me now. No-one watches when I dance.

Howe They pass by, hooded and muffled against the infecting air, with no word of greeting. What a fine hot summer to die in!

Bedlam They melt in silence, like wax.

Howe June the twenty-second.

William Thornley enters pushing a wheelbarrow; in it, dead, half-wrapped in an old sheet, is Edward Thornley. Mary Thornley follows, wrapped in a black cloak

Howe Edward Thornley. The soldier who refused to run.

Bedlam He was strong. He shooed me away when I sang on Sundays.

Howe Wheeled half-naked to an undignified trench. He was a soldier once, in the army at Marston. Now he's filling for a grave . . . July began with a rainstorm. The roads were all steaming.

Bedlam Flowers grew in the streets, didn't they.

Howe Then, the sixth day.

Inside one of the cottage areas, Elizabeth Swanne falls to the ground and remains lying there

Elizabeth Swanne, aged twenty, living alone, a virgin, in virtuous and prayerful solitude. No-one knew when she died.

Bedlam Except me. I saw her dead in the fireplace. I looked in her open eyes.

Howe No-one came to close them.

We see Mary Thornley sprawled across a table

And at dinnertime, Mary Thornley, with bread in her mouth. She was lucky. Her brother buried her, ignoring his headache.

William Thornley takes her over his shoulder and carries her out

But who will bury him, left alone in his bed? Two days and five people later, the next.

Edytha Torre is carried along the street by shoulders and ankles by John and Thomas Torre. She is wrapped in what is clearly a carefully preserved shroud, and her hands and feet protrude and trail in the dirt

Edytha Torre, plain faced and loving.

Bedlam Granny.

Howe Sixty-five years, ending in an open field.

Bedlam She gave me bread.

They watch her carried off

Howe The living close their minds to all but survival. Locked like prisoners in this circle, we wait for the executioner's finger. No-one has run away. A hundred and thirty-eight of us will stay here forever.

Lydia Chapman walks weakly on, supporting herself on a wall. She stops, and sinks down, back to the wall, exhausted. She becomes still

A hundred and thirty-nine—Lydia Chapman was left with a baby when she was young, but the father never returned and the child died. Her face grew sharp, and her tongue bitter. Now her smothered desires lie still, among nettles and new grass and moon daisies . . .

Bedlam I seen a man on a door.
Howe Have you?
Bedlam And a bundle of washing with legs.
Howe The dead must be buried somehow, boy.
Bedlam And a woman in a chair being carried like a queen.
Howe Going to bed in comfort . . .
Bedlam I like the sun. It keeps me warm.
Howe Well, it's August, boy. Harvest time. And seventy-three of us buried since the doors were closed . . .

The stage is now empty, except for Elizabeth Swanne and Lydia Chapman, still lying where they fell

Look at those two, boy.
Bedlam They're dead.
Howe There are no relatives to come for them.
Bedlam Leave them till autumn when the leaves fall.
Howe Are you frightened, boy?
Bedlam Only of dogs with big teeth.
Howe Then go and find a shovel. And let's start digging.

Howe hoists up both women, one on to each shoulder, and walks off, with their heads and hands dangling behind him, followed by the Bedlam

Music, as the villagers enter in ones and twos, and stand in separated small groups around the stage. They consist of the following characters: Mrs Cooper, Thomas and Frances Torre, all seven Friths, George Mower, Howe and Unwin. They are all more or less in rags. Mompesson and Catherine come in to them, as though to conduct the service in the open air, and stand with their heads bowed as the villagers assemble. Mompesson looks drawn and ill. Stanley enters downstage, observing the service, but apart from it. He speaks as the group assembles

Stanley We have come to this now. Our church is the green Dell, with the sky for a roof; our pulpit a cave, and our graveyard the open field. The bare bones of worship, for the remainder, who still cling on to life.

Mompesson raises his head from prayer

Mompesson Brothers and sisters, I ask your prayers for those who were with us here at our last meeting, and are now with God.
Stanley In the ground.
Mompesson For Margaret Allen, John Torre, Samuel Ealott, Rowland

Mower, Thomas Barkinge, Nicholas Whitby, Jonathan Talbot, Mary Whitby, Rowland Mower the elder, Sarah Ealott, Joseph Allen, Ann Mortin, Robert Kemp, George Ashe, Mary Nealor, John Hadfield, Robert Buxton, Ann Naylor, Jonathan Naylor, Elizabeth Glover, Alexander Hadfield, Jane Nealor and Godfrey Torre, whom God's hand has taken from us in the last week, I ask your prayers, and Christ's love in intercession.

Silence

Stanley English names in a book.
Mompesson Today I am conscious of a question that is in all our minds.
Stanley There is a question in my mind, too. A terrible question.
Mompesson How much more can God ask of us?

Stanley remains silent

But my answer must be the same as it has always been. There is no end, by our reckoning. We have already endured beyond any man's expectation, and we may have to suffer worse things yet.
Stanley We are beggars now, even our rhetoric is wearing thin.
Mompesson We can feel those nails that tore Christ's hands. We are nailed to a village, as he was to a tree. A long day he hung there, and it seemed that the sun would never set. He cried, as we are crying now, "Father, why hast thou forsaken me?" . . . Why hast thou forsaken me . . . ?

Stanley seems about to speak, but he lowers his head, too. The second cry is a personal one from Mompesson and the whole silent village, and cannot be answered. Mompesson speaks quietly and tremulously

Yet for seven weeks something has kept us here. Faith that this is the right thing to do, or whatever we call it that stops us from running when we wake each morning. Cling on to that. Lock up your hearts, even to love, till the time comes when we can open them again. That way we will go on.
Stanley In the beginning, it was an ideal, but that's forgotten now. For a man on the rack, endurance becomes an end in itself.
Mompesson We must pray for more strength yet, and that God's mercy will not be long in coming.

They lower their heads

Stanley This is the hardest time. Life is the length of one day, and a repeated daily question: will it be me tomorrow?

Everything seems frozen in this moment of bleak despair, the darkest moment in the play

Slowly the villagers begin to leave, one by one, with little acknowledgement of each other

Stanley comes over to where Catherine and Mompesson still stand together, watching the departing villagers

Well, Mompesson?

Mompesson What?

Stanley Is your mind still as clear as it was?

Mompesson I think it's gone cold. We aren't people any more. We're figures in a sum. What do you think?

Stanley Nothing.

Mompesson There's something you keep hidden. What is it?

Stanley Blankness.

Catherine Our resolution is firm. Are you weakening?

Stanley No.

Mompesson What then?

Stanley A question.

Mompesson What?

Stanley When this mountain of dead men is measured, what answer shall we give, you and I?

To which question there is no answer

  Stanley turns slowly and walks away

Mompesson and Catherine remain

Catherine Don't listen. You spoke well today.

Mompesson Speaking is easy.

Catherine They look to you for their strength.

Mompesson I am the weakest, by far! For a while what we were doing seemed right. Now I don't care.

Catherine You must care!

Mompesson It doesn't matter. In my own mind I am sure now we will all die. No-one will be spared.

Catherine We have been spared.

Mompesson Mere chance. Our turn is not yet.

Catherine It's a strange thing, I feel full of confidence. Since we sent the children away . . .

Mompesson Don't speak of that!

Catherine I told you it would make us strong.

Mompesson It has torn me to shreds! The guilt has been heavy with me since the day they went. What we attempted is already defeated. It's no wonder my words sound hollow. They are mere words. We keep our records and we wait our turn. That's all.

Catherine William!

Mompesson That's all!

Mompesson moves quickly off without looking round. Sadly and slowly Catherine follows him

Marshall Howe enters briskly, with a body over his shoulders tied up in coarse sacking. Female hands and hair protrude from the neck of the sack. He is accompanied by the Bedlam who carries his shovel

Howe So much for the Friths, eh, boy? Them and the Hancocks reckoned they were immortal last week.
Bedlam They're all dead now though.
Howe The Hancocks are all dead, lad, I know that. Dead and buried in Riley field.
Bedlam I watched the lady digging the holes. I was hiding behind the wall and she didn't see. She cried and cried, and it made me laugh.
Howe Ay, Mrs Hancock, poor love, with her husband, three daughters and three sons to bury. They say she's run mad with it, and I wouldn't be surprised, would you, son?

Howe sits down on the bench, bumping the body down with no ceremony. Bedlam crouches beside it

Bedlam I don't run mad.
Howe You're barmy, lad, that's why. You've got a head start on the rest of us.

The Bedlam laughs foolishly

And now it's the Friths' turn, you see? She's the fourth of them in two weeks. Old George, he won't touch them. Calls for me instead. I've used sheets, and doors, and chairs and blankets. Now I'm down to sacking. Still: it's better than burying them naked.

Unwin comes round a corner, or perhaps sticks his head out of a window, if available, before entering fully

Unwin Not the way you do it it isn't! Do you have to come and gossip under my window when I'm trying to have a snooze?
Howe Hallo, Unwin, I thought you were dead weeks ago.
Unwin You thought wrong then, didn't you. I've been keeping meself to meself. Who's that?
Howe Well, she was Elizabeth Frith yesterday. She's a lump of meat in a sack today.
Unwin You've got no respect, have you.
Howe Should I have? You try smelling her.
Unwin I've heard about you stealing.
Howe I collect my wages, that's all. A few pennies or a bit of pewter from the empty houses.
Unwin It's wicked to steal from the dead.
Howe I'll have your pipe and tobacco tin when your turn comes.
Unwin You won't bury me!
Howe If I don't, no-one will.
Unwin If you touch that pipe, I'll be back and haunt you, and that's a promise. How's your wife?

Howe All right.

Unwin And your son Billy?

Howe Well.

Unwin What you going to steal from them, eh?

Howe You mind what you say, you old villain, or I'll leave you to rot! God won't have you if you stink.

Unwin An' he won't have you, neither, he's got other plans for you!

Howe If you're not rotten already. Even the plague turns his nose up!

Unwin begins to go, then stops and watches Howe as he prepares to lift up the body

Unwin Give her a prayer, then, for the good of your soul.

Howe I don't exactly pray. But I lean on my shovel, and I shout out good and loud, "Right ho, old Nick, now you keep away from here, or I'll be after you!" Good enough, I reckon.

Unwin You're a heathen, ain't you.

Howe No more than most . . . Here, do you know how many this makes?

Unwin Too many, I know that.

Howe Two hundred and five, since the day it started.

Unwin Ah, I believe it.

Howe And a hundred and nineteen of 'em since we shut ourselves in. Life used to be good here. You know what it is now, don't you?

Unwin What?

Howe A short trot to the nearest grave.

Unwin Ah, well, I don't need waking up to be told that, do I!

Unwin goes off

Howe watches him, laughing. The Bedlam comes and sits close to him

Bedlam I think everyone will die.

Howe Do you then.

Bedlam Except me.

Howe Why not you?

Bedlam I frighten him. Because of my bad leg.

Howe Oh aye?

Bedlam I saw him sitting in a tree. But I made a bad face and he flew away.

Howe That was a bird.

Bedlam He had big wings and made shadows everywhere.

Howe looks at the boy, then stoops and shoulders the body

Howe Com on, Liz. We'll find you a nice comfortable hole where you can rot in peace.

Howe exits carrying the body, followed by the Bedlam

Mompesson and Catherine come slowly on from opposite sides of the stage. Mompesson sits down in a dazed manner, and Catherine joins him. They both look ragged, dirty and desperately tired. There are blood and vomit stains on Catherine's apron. Both are emotionally drained

Mompesson Is it finished?

Catherine Yes. She died peacefully.

Mompesson She is to be envied. A peaceful death must seem luxury after this daily agony.

Catherine It must seem so. Yes.

Mompesson I never thought it could be as bad as this. Not in nightmares, or visions of the damned in Hell. There can be nothing worse. We are in the pit.

Catherine It doesn't seem possible in the midst of such beauty and emptiness. Miles of naked hillside with never a man in sight, so solid and unshakeable. Are we really dying?

Mompesson Fifty-six this month. In nineteen days.

Catherine It's very strange to be alive in a certain place, and then gone, and the place unaltered, as if you had never been there. I can't imagine it.

Mompesson Remember some of our dead. Richard Sydall and his children. Old Humphrey Torre and his family. The Thornleys. They'll convince you.

A silence. Then she looks at him

Catherine William—I ought to tell you.

Mompesson What?

Catherine I have a headache. And a sweet smell in my nose.

Silence

Mompesson (*drained*) No.

Catherine Yes. I know it well enough by now.

Mompesson (*quietly*) Dear God . . .

Catherine So we had better go to the rectory.

Mompesson Dear Father, you can't do that to me . . .

Catherine There are things I must do and arrangements to make. I should like to die calmly and in comfort.

Mompesson Catherine!

Catherine No anguish, William. We're long past that. Calmly and soberly. We've seen it often enough to know how best to manage. Come on. The sooner I'm in bed the better.

Catherine rises and walks off a little uncertainly

Mompesson watches her go as though hypnotized. He half follows her, then falls on his knees c

Mompesson (*loudly, anguished*) You can't do that! God, Father, you can't do that to me!

The Lights fade around him, till he is kneeling in a pool of light, with only the cyclorama lit behind him

Stanley enters at the back of the stage, and walks slowly across it behind Mompesson during the following section

Their meeting is not a naturalistic one that can be defined in terms of time and place. It is a meeting of their private terrors and thoughts, not their physical bodies. Mompesson remains kneeling throughout

Stanley We can't go much further now. People can bear so much.

Mompesson And then they crack?

Stanley Yes.

Mompesson How much can they bear?

Stanley We've seen what they have borne. How much more is a question.

Mompesson The pit is wide open. But we won't fall now, will we? Not after so long.

Stanley I don't know. And perhaps that doesn't matter any more.

Stanley walks slowly and thoughtfully off

Mompesson is more emotional than we have ever seen him, half-crazed with grief and fear

Mompesson After so long and so much endured, we won't fall now. We will stay here, till the last one dies, if need be. Till the last one dies!

Behind Mompesson, visible only as a cloaked silhouette, George Mower enters, and points an accusing finger at him

George Mower August the twentieth, sixteen sixty-six. Elizabeth Frith, Margaret Mortin, Ann Rowland, Joan Buxton. All dead of the plague!

Mompesson Till the last one dies!

George Mower remains pointing at Mompesson

Frances Torre enters likewise and points

Frances Torre August the twenty-first, sixteen sixty-six. Francis Frith and Ruth Mortin. Both dead of the plague!

Mompesson Till the last one dies!

Frances Torre remains pointing

Thomas Torre enters likewise, and points at Mompesson

Thomas Torre August the twenty-second, sixteen sixty-six. A baby Frith, unchristened, and Lydia Kempe. Both dead of the plague!

Mompesson Till the last one dies!

Thomas Torre remains pointing

Mary Frith enters likewise, and points

Mary Frith August the twenty-third, sixteen sixty-six. Peter Hall of Bretton. Dead of the plague!
Mompesson Till the last one dies!

Mary Frith remains pointing

George Frith enters likewise, and points

George Frith August the twenty-fourth, sixteen sixty-six. Granny Mortin, dead of the plague!
Mompesson Till the last one dies!

The five black figures are now all standing pointing to the kneeling Mompesson

Marshall Howe enters downstage, on the opposite side to Mompesson, and points like the rest

Howe August the twenty-fifth, sixteen sixty-six. Who will die today?

The Lights suddenly change so that only Marshall Howe is visible downstage

The Bedlam enters and joins him

Bedlam Have you heard the news?
Howe What news?
Bedlam A lady's dying.
Howe That's not news, boy. News is something that's different from usual, like "nobody's died today". Anyway, I've heard about Annie Frith.
Bedlam It's not her.
Howe Someone else, is it?
Bedlam The frail lady. The pretty one who gave me the coat.
Howe The rector's wife?
Bedlam The lady from the church . . .
Howe Then God help us all. One of our props is falling.

Howe and the Bedlam exit together

The Lights come up to show Mompesson kneeling by Catherine's bed, with Frances Torre standing near by in attendance. The villagers are standing, as though waiting downstairs in the rectory hall for news. They stand, or walk about, or sit, conscious that they are in the rector's house. Those present are Mrs Cooper, George Frith, Mary Frith, George Mower, Thomas Torre and Unwin. As Mompesson begins to pray Frances Torre leaves the bedroom and moves to join the others. Catherine's responses are weak, and get progressively weaker

Mompesson Oh Lord, save thy servant.

Catherine Which putteth her trust in thee.

Mompesson Send her help from the holy place.

Catherine And ever more mightily defend her.

Mrs Cooper What will the rector do, poor young man?

George Frith What we've all done. My Annie died this morning. Only two of us left now, eh, Mary?

Mary Frith Yes, Dad.

Thomas Torre My sister's in there with them.

George Mower That's dangerous.

Thomas Torre After what she's done for us? Nine of my family are dead, and she was with every one.

George Mower Ah, but she's like that, isn't she?

Unwin We've had it a year. Too late now to worry.

George Frith This time last year we was getting ready for the wake.

Mrs Cooper When that black box came to my house.

Unwin Ah.

Frances Torre enters to the rest

George Mower How is she?

Frances Torre She's dying. He's saying the prayers.

The Lights concentrate again on Mompesson and Catherine, and the others become silhouettes

Mompesson Let the enemy have no advantage of her.

Catherine Nor the wicked approach to hurt her.

Mompesson Be unto her, O Lord, a strong tower.

Catherine From the face of her enemy.

Mompesson O Lord, hear our prayer.

Catherine does not answer

O Lord, hear our prayer . . .

Silence. The tension mounts as he waits for her reply. But it does not come. Mompesson's head falls forward on to her body. The Lights fall a few points on the villagers, and concentrate on Mompesson fallen over his wife's body. After a few seconds, Mompesson stirs. He gets up with an intense weary slowness, slowly lifts the sheet up, and lets it fall over Catherine's face. It is a gesture of absolute finality. Then he turns away from her, in a daze

Now—now—now. What must I do? I've seen this before. But then it was some other man's wife. What did they do when it happened? The moment when it happened? Nothing. They did nothing. They were turned to stone, they were wax, they melted tears . . . No—that's not it— I must write letters. I must write letters to the children. I must tell them their mother is dead . . . My wife is dead . . . (*All restraint cracks*) Christ, Jesus, Father, how can I forgive you for this? I gave you my whole life in service, I was burning in my love and desire to do your work. My most precious cup I gave into your keeping, and you took a hammer and smashed it. Must I go down on my knees and pick up the

fragments, and thank you for your mercy? What did I do that was evil
to deserve this? Yes, God, we are all sinners, we are all weak, and we
do wrong. But to condemn us wholesale, to kill us thousands at a
blow, to tread us into the earth like flies or insects that are worth no
more, is that your love and mercy? Do you stand us up like a child
with tin soldiers only to knock us down, with no choice or justice? I
have seen things here no Christian would believe . . . My wife would
rebuke me for this. She would put her hand on my arm and restrain
me from these madmen's ravings. We can beat forever on the walls of
life. The room is confined and square. There is only one way out. I
sent my children away. Everyone else stayed. I spoke of ideals, and
rightness, and endurance for good. But that was hypocrisy and lying.
It is paid for now.

*The Lights rise on the villagers as he moves across to them. There is a
silence as he confronts them*

I have a confession to make to you . . . I have been a traitor to your
suffering. I sent . . .

Mrs Cooper We knew all along about your children, Rector.

Pause. Mompesson is staggered

Mompesson You knew?

Mrs Cooper Right from the first. Old Unwin saw you creep out of the
door with them at midnight, looking so guilty.

Unwin I was out for a walk I was.

Mompesson But you said nothing?

Mrs Cooper They were only babies. We'd have done the same.

Mompesson I betrayed your trust.

Mrs Cooper Well, perhaps you did, if you look at it like that. But you
loved us with all your heart, too, in the hardest way. Not with words.
With actions.

Mompesson I loved you?

Mrs Cooper You did what you could to keep us alive. No man can do more
than that.

Mompesson But . . .

Mrs Cooper We forgave the rest months ago. All our prayers are with you
in your grief.

Whole Group Amen.

The villagers go off together, leaving Mompesson alone

Mompesson I loved them? I felt nothing . . . And they forgive me, with
what might be their last breath . . . I don't understand.

*Stanley enters to him, and they stand together looking down at Catherine's
body*

Stanley Mompesson—I wanted to speak my sorrow.

Mompesson She is another name in the book now. August the twenty-fifth, Catherine Mompesson.

Stanley You bear it well.

Mompesson There is no other way to bear it.

Stanley I was afraid . . .

Mompesson You need not be. Nothing has changed. The shadow has not lifted yet, and we will go on as before.

Stanley We must now.

Mompesson Yes. I haven't visited the villagers today. Will you come with me?

Stanley Yes, I'll come.

Mompesson Let's go then. There are not many left to visit, but they are all worth our prayers.

Mompesson and Stanley go off together. A short pause. Marshall Howe enters, carrying a spade. He walks c and stops. He throws the spade to the ground. A loud clang. He does not move

Howe There's an end to all my gardening. I've seen so many of them, dying and in pain; and at the end of it, I've buried them, but it didn't move me. It was a job to be done by someone. I never thought it could happen to me.

The Bedlam comes running in, excited

Bedlam Marshall Howe, Marshall Howe!

Howe Not today, boy.

Bedlam You must come, Marshall Howe. There's another one left all alone.

Howe Who is it this time?

Bedlam The old man.

Howe Which old man?

Bedlam Not the one who went away, the other one.

Howe Unwin?

Bedlam That's it. Nunwin. He's lying on the floor, and he's dead.

Howe Unwin dead? It must be the end of the world.

Bedlam Come on, Marshall Howe!

Howe I've finished with digging now, boy.

Bedlam Come on!

Howe Sixty or seventy I've buried. One every day, and some days two or three. I never cared. I wasn't frightened to touch the scabby bodies. I was too strong for it. But my wife died three days ago.

Bedlam Where have you been, Marshall Howe, I haven't seen you?

Howe I made that grave, too. Mechanically, like the others. But I couldn't throw the earth in. I stood there for half an hour, just looking at her in the hole.

Bedlam Sometimes we sing, Marshall Howe, don't we, and you shovel, and I use my hands.

Howe Aye, lad, we do. But my son Billy died this morning. So there'll be no more digging now.

Bedlam Don't cry, Marshall Howe. I don't like it when you cry.

Howe No, lad. Come on then. I promised that old devil I'd bury him, so I'd better be good as my word.

Bedlam And we'll sing, too! Like before!

Howe Aye, we'll sing, lad. If you like. (*He picks up the shovel*)

Howe and the Bedlam go out together. Stanley enters by himself

Stanley Today is death's birthday. One year ago today George Vicars died. Two hundred and thirty-six of us are dead since that day . . . It seems that we must all die, down to the last man, before the pestilence will be satisfied. Perhaps it is wrong to do things for the right reasons. Our motives, never so good nor honest, seem to mean nothing. The end is always the same failure. We dreamed of honesty and self sacrifice, and when we woke, we saw only dead meat. How is it then that I feel that something is still living here, something uncommon, and hard to find in the day-to-day traffic of men? Each day I feel it stronger. A refusal to settle for less than the possible; an assertion of identity, a spiritual strength that lingers in the empty cottages and deserted farmyards. In spite of the dead, and for the second time in my life, a sense of community . . . (*He sinks on to a bench in thought*)

The Lights reveal on the other side of the stage the interior of Unwin's cottage, with Howe and Bedlam just entering. The cottage is full of all kinds of junk, and Unwin himself lies sprawled on the floor

Bedlam There he is, Marshall Howe.

Howe (*crossing and crouching by him*) Ay, there you are, you poor old devil. Old Nick got you at last, has he? Well. Not before time.

Bedlam Shall we bury him in the garden?

Howe Hang on a minute, lad, hang on! I'm looking for something.

Bedlam What is it, Marshall Howe, tell me?

Howe You just wait and see, son. Something special. Something he owes me.

Howe and Bedlam go to the far side of the room, searching, and throwing Unwin's junk all over the place. Unwin opens one eye. Quietly, unheard, he gets to his feet. He looks at the backs of the two searchers. Howe finds what he is looking for

Unwin You put that pipe down!

Both men jump out of their skins when they turn and see Unwin on his feet

Howe Good God!

Unwin Ah, I caught you, didn't I!

Howe Get back on the floor, you're supposed to be dead!

Unwin Well I'm not, so there! Flesh and blood that is, bit scrawny, but flesh and blood all the same. Give me that pipe!

Howe You were definitely dead. I saw you.

Unwin Ay, well, I may have been. And then again I may not have been. Maybe I was just having a rest.

Howe Cold you were. Like ice.

Unwin Course I was cold, it's September, ain't it? You'll be cold when you get to my age. If you should be so lucky.

Bedlam I thought you were dead, Nunwin.

Unwin Ah, that'll be the day. You can put up the shutters when that day comes. Listen, boy. Next time you come to my cottage and see me stretched out on the floor, you don't run round the village shouting "Old Unwin's dead! Old Unwin's dead!" You shout, "I *think* old Unwin's dead!"

Howe Well, if it's good enough for Jesus, Unwin, it's good enough for you, eh?

Unwin That's blasphemy, Marshall Howe, and you know it! Are you going to sit there talking all day, or are you going to get me a drink?

Howe Are you sure you feel well enough for a drink?

Unwin When I don't you can start digging!

Howe crosses over from the house area towards where Stanley is still seated on the bench. The Lights come up at the bench, as Unwin and Bedlam follow Howe

Howe Eh, cheer up, Mr Stanley, I've got some good news. Or then again, it might be bad news, depends how you look at it.

Stanley What news is that?

Howe Old Unwin's just come back from the dead!

Howe roars with laughter and marches off stage, followed by the protesting Unwin, and the excited Bedlam

Stanley smiles, and then speaks quietly to himself

Stanley Back from the dead . . .

Stanley gets up slowly and walks off

A few seconds pass in absolute silence. Then there is a sudden and loud peal of church bells and the Lights come up to full day

Slowly, patiently, Mrs Cooper comes on and sits on the bench. She is followed, entering one by one, by Frances Torre, George Mower, Unwin, Howe and the Bedlam, and last of all, Mary Frith. They enter from different directions, slowly and wonderingly. They look more like refugees from a battle or survivors from a concentration camp than villagers. They are dirty and in rags, and their faces are haunted by the daily presence of death

Frances Torre What's happening?

Mary Frith Why is the bell ringing?

Mrs Cooper Mr Stanley's in there with the rector. They've been talking an hour. It must be over.

Mary Frith Over?

George Mower Over?

Frances Torre Over?

Howe It can't be over. We're still alive.

A pause. The bell stops. They listen to the silence

Mary Frith (*quietly*) There's one thing I can't get used to, Mrs Cooper.

Mrs Cooper You can get used to anything, Mary.

Mary Frith I can't get used to living alone. It's not a big cottage, but it's so empty. There used to be seven of us.

Slowly, in the silence, Stanley enters. He stops and they all look at him

Stanley I have been speaking to the rector. For two weeks, since Joseph Mortin died on October the fourteenth, we have all been waiting for the next one. There has been no next one so far. So it looks like the plague is over . . .

A completely blank pause. Nothing

Stanley Tomorrow there will be work for us all. Today is for thanksgiving, and remembrance. God bless you, good people.

Silence. Nothing. Slowly they all drift off stage, leaving Stanley still standing c, and Mrs Cooper and George Mower still seated on benches

Mrs Cooper rises wearily and crosses to Stanley. George Mower does not move

Mrs Cooper Where's the rector, Mr Stanley?

Stanley I—asked him to come with me to speak to you. But he preferred to stay in the rectory.

Mrs Cooper Is he well?

Stanley He's in better health now. But company, even our company, distresses him.

Mrs Cooper Poor man . . .

Mrs Cooper goes slowly off

Stanley sees George Mower still sitting by himself, and crosses over to him

Stanley We must live again, George. We have no choice.

George Mower I don't know what to do, Mr Stanley. I can't think any more.

Stanley Well, come round the village with me, George, and we will think what has to be done.

George Mower Will you help me, sir?

Stanley We will help each other.

George Mower and Stanley go off

The stage is empty for a few seconds

Unwin comes on, taking long and satisfying draughts from his clay pipe, and smiling at the world in general. After a few seconds Andrew Merril enters. The two men see each other, and stop dead, without saying anything

Unwin Good day, Andrew Merril.
Merril Good day, Unwin.
Unwin I was hoping you'd be dead and buried by now.
Merril I was sure you would be.
Unwin Well I'm not, so there.
Merril Neither am I, so there.
Unwin Shall I tell you why you survived, Merril?
Merril Because I took steps, that's why.
Unwin The plague knows a bad bargain when he sees one.
Merril And shall I tell you why you survived, Unwin?
Unwin Will power, in here!
Merril Even old Nick draws the line somewhere!

Unwin and Merril turn angrily from each other, and march off in opposite directions

For a few seconds the stage is empty

Rowland Torre enters, slowly, on to the vast and empty stage

Rowland Emmot! . . . Emmot! . . . Where are you? It's me, Rowland . . .!
Silence. He walks around the stage, then stops

Nothing. Are they all dead? I heard the bell, and I galloped like a madman. But this is beyond belief. There are flowers and weeds in the street, a foot high! But no people. She must be here somewhere. At the house, the door's off the hinge, and there's grass growing through the cracks in the flags. It takes a long time for grass to grow . . . She must be here somewhere . . . All we had to do was wait . . . Emmot! Emmot!

Frances Torre enters, carrying a bundle of old clothes

Rowland does not see her

Frances Torre Hallo, Rowland.

He spins round and stares at her for a long time

Rowland Emmot . . . ? No.

Frances Torre It's me, Frances.

Rowland For a moment I thought . . . Have you seen her?

Frances Torre Who?

Rowland Emmot Sydall. You remember, we were going to be married . . .

Frances Torre Oh yes. A long time ago.

Rowland A few months ago, that's all.

Frances Torre Her mother lives up in the Delph. In a cave I think.

Rowland In a cave . . . ? Is Emmot with her?

Frances Torre Emmot? She's dead.

Rowland When?

Frances Torre When? I can't remember dates. You'll find her in the rector's book with all the others. The end of April, I think . . .

Frances trails out with her bundle. She has spoken more like a walking shadow than a person

Rowland All that time ago. Hardly a week after I went . . . I must go to her mother. This place is a graveyard.

Rowland walks slowly off. Mompesson enters reading a letter. Stanley enters to him. Mompesson looks up, and for a moment they look at each other

Stanley It's over then.

Mompesson Yes. Over.

Stanley It's strange. Few men, in all the time that's gone, can have seen so much together, or been pressed so hard. And yet . . .

Mompesson What?

Stanley We've never been friends.

Mompesson It depends what that means.

Stanley What the world means. Friends. Perhaps that was asking too much.

Mompesson We live in a bad time. Man is set against man.

Stanley Didn't we change that?

Mompesson We ignored it. It's still there. Age, background, belief. We worship the same God, but . . .

Stanley Different faces . . . I have never been a scholar. I was born among the people, and I have always been their man.

Mompesson I envy you for that. There is no book written that I cannot unravel. Except the writing in a man's heart. That's a language I still can't read. What I do understand, I construe clumsily. God gave me this mind, more than to most men. I am trapped within it.

Stanley You are young yet.

Mompesson Old in pity, Stanley. After what we've seen. I wanted to change so much. Now I only want to sympathize.

Stanley Yes, I understand.

Mompesson I thought I was God's soldier. Now I am a witness at the tomb. Nothing more.

Stanley There is only one thing then.

Mompesson To be separate again, as before.

Stanley Yes.

Pause. Mompesson shows him the letter, and tries to assume a brisker, more prosaic tone

Mompesson There is a letter here. From the Duke. No-one has died of the plague in Derbyshire, except here, in Eyam.

Stanley We succeeded then.

Mompesson Apparently.

Stanley We did a great thing, Mompesson. I am sure in my own mind now. Many people died. Five-sixths were sacrificed. But we were right to act as we did.

Mompesson I suppose so.

Stanley For you it is harder to say it. But you will see one day. We set our sights uncompromisingly at the highest, and we hit the mark. You are right to pity. If nothing, we deserve that. But there is this, too. That for once, men's acts matched their imagination. That the greatest things that can be conceived of men can sometimes be acted, too. We proved it here.

Mompesson I can see nothing but the dead.

A pause

Stanley We must say good-bye then.

Mompesson Our paths are by nature opposite. For a moment only they crossed.

Pause

Stanley God be with you then.

Mompesson And you.

The two men look at each other for a second, then Stanley rises with decision, and walks briskly off. Mompesson remains. Around him the remaining villagers begin the task of clearing up the village, sweeping, throwing out old mattresses and clothes and sheets for a bonfire. Unwin and Merril are much in evidence, and perhaps Stanley says a few words before going off

It is a scene of silent activity, contrasted with Mompesson's reflective still-ness

Slowly—uncertainly—as the autumn of the year sixteen sixty-six became winter, our village came back to life. The unbelieving survivors gradually learned how to speak to each other again, to love, marry, work and bear children and live as people normally do. Perhaps they were more conscious than some of the shadow we all live under. Or perhaps they too forgot all they had learned and endured, and lived from day to day, as though life were endless, and death no more than a bad dream . . . Stanley left the village that winter, and died, I believe, soon after. I left, too, after a few years, taking my children with me, to a new parish in Norfolk.

The two Children come on stage to him. He rises and stands with his hands on their shoulders

I suppose I once had greater ambitions, but they died here, among the rest. I dream my days away now, in pastoral quietude. Somewhere where what is demanded of me is not more than I can bear.

By now the stage behind Mompesson has cleared of all except Howe and the Bedlam. He goes off with his two children

Howe and the Bedlam come forward together to meet c. The empty stage stretches out behind them, and we are aware of the numbers of people who have populated it, and are now gone. Quiet music is heard

Howe Hallo, boy.
Bedlam Where's your spade?
Howe The digging's finished now.
Bedlam What shall we do, then?
Howe Live again. Begin to admire it, as we did before. With eyes that know its value, because they have seen death's land.
Bedlam Where's that?
Howe It was here. Remember?
Bedlam I remember all those bodies we buried.
Howe They were people once.
Bedlam Nobody buried me, though.
Howe You're not worth it, are you. Bones all the wrong shape, scabs in your hair. Not worth the trouble.
Bedlam And you're too big.
Howe Ah.
Bedlam What are you doing?
Howe Watching the night come. Coming like a thief, with no noise and no disturbance, in the usual way. Let's be quiet now, boy. We'll stand here, watching the lamps go out, till it's all quiet, and peaceful, and dark.

The music comes to a slow climax and we see the two figures, the giant and the cripple, silhouetted against the empty wastes of the stage

The Lights fade, as—

the CURTAIN *slowly falls*

FURNITURE AND PROPERTY LIST

ACT I

On stage: MAIN AREA
Large stone cross on rostrum
One or two benches and seats

COTTAGE AREA
Bed and bedding
Chairs
Clothes-rail
Bucket

RECTORY AREA
Table. *On it:* candle, book
3 chairs

Off stage: Tin with coins, handbell **(Bedlam)**
Large black box with clothing and draperies **(Carter)**

ACT II

Strike: Everything from cottage except bed
Off stage: 3 coffins **(Villagers)**
Bible **(Stanley)**
Piece of string **(Bedlam)**
Basket **(Catherine)**
Bags and cases **(Bradshaws)**
Bundles and bags **(Villagers)**

ACT III

Strike: All luggage
Set: Bottle on bench (for **Unwin**)
Piles of junk, including clay pipe, in **Unwin's** cottage
Off stage: Various buckets, wheelbarrows, trolleys, etc. **(Villagers)**
Wheelbarrow and sheet **(William Thornley)**
Shroud **(Torre Family)**
Spade **(Howe)**
Bundle of old clothes **(Frances Torre)**
Letter **(Mompesson)**
Various brooms, mattresses, old sheets, clothes, personal belongings
(Villagers)

LIGHTING PLOT

Property fittings required: nil
Exterior and interiors on open stage. The same scenes throughout

ACT I

To open: Rear lighting to silhouette village anc cross

ACT II

To open: General lighting to suggest daylight

EFFECTS PLOT

ACT I

MADE AND PRINTED IN GREAT BRITAIN BY
LATIMER TREND & COMPANY LTD, PLYMOUTH
MADE IN ENGLAND